MASTER FISHERMAN

CARP

KEVIN CLIFFORD

MASTER FISHERMAN

CARP

KEVIN CLIFFORD

WARD LOCK

First published in Great Britain in 1989
by Ward Lock Limited, Artillery House, Artillery Row,
London SW1P 1RT, a Cassell Company

Designed by Ann Thompson
Edited by Richard Dawes
Illustrations by Peter Bull Art

Text filmset 12 on 13½pt Times Roman
by Fakenham Photosetting Limited, Fakenham, Norfolk
Printed in Great Britain at The Bath Press, Avon

British Library Cataloguing in Publication Data
Clifford, Kevin
Carp. – (Master fishermen).
1. Carp. Angling
I. Title II. Series
799.1′752

ISBN 0–7063–6790–1

CONTENTS

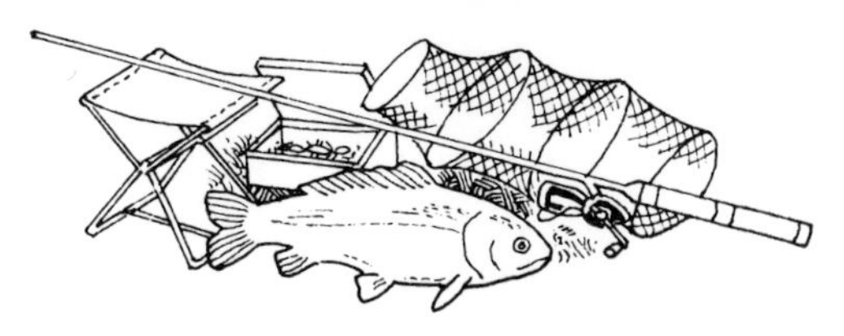

FOREWORD

As a short visit to the tackle store will prove, carp fishing has taken off beyond all our wildest dreams. There are hundreds – it could be thousands – of specialized carp rods now available. Reels with built-in bite alarms. And enough prepacked, different-coloured and flavoured ready-made boiled baits to give most human beings, let alone the fish, trouble in distinguishing one from another.

Where is it all leading? I wish I knew. But what I do know is, more carp anglers would actually catch the fish they seek, were they to first read a book like this. With the help of specialist guest writers, Kevin has achieved an interesting balance of expert advice. *Master Fisherman: Carp* is an excellent starting-point for those who have yet to catch many carp, and I was delighted when he asked me to write the foreword.

Unlike many of today's big names in carp fishing, Kevin is essentially an all-rounder, who has under his belt success with a whole list of other species, from big chub to her ladyship the grayling. He trots for roach, waits out for reservoir bream, deadbaits for big pike, and swimfeeds for tench. This gives him, and anyone who reads this book, the edge, in that much of the watercraft and technique used to catch other species is equally effective for putting carp on the bank.

Kevin and I first met back in the mid-1970s, not while carp fishing but through sharing many tench sessions on an estate lake in North Norfolk. Fishing corn and worms with a swimfeeder was then the most effective method, resulting in tench of over 7 lb (3 kg), and many five- and six-pounders (2·25 kg and 2·7 kg) for us both. But float fishing can, in the right circumstances, also account for big tench, or big anything, especially big carp. Yet so few carp anglers today even own a float, let alone know how to use one. I was specially pleased, therefore, that Kevin has dwelt on this technique and on numerous other basic but important skills. An angling apprenticeship like this serves everyone well, be their choice putting a stick float down the Trent or waiting for the buzzer to sound.

I particularly liked Kevin's introduction to the history and spread of the carp throughout Asia and Europe, and his description of the modern species and its environment. Carp culture goes back a very long way, and I believe it is important to be aware of how it all began. Good reading and good carp fishing.

JOHN WILSON *February 1989*

CHAPTER ONE

CARP FISHING TODAY

Many of today's carp fishermen believe that the modern concept of carp fishing began with Richard Walker and the Carp Catchers' Club in the early 1950s. By modern concept I mean the belief that it is possible to catch carp by intention and not rely totally on good fortune. While it can be fairly claimed that Dick and his colleagues popularized carp fishing, and invented and developed various aspects of the sport, it would be wrong to discount the achievements and contributions made by their predecessors, such as Otto Overbeck, J. C. S. Mummery, E. Burton and B. B. (Denys Watkins-Pitchford). Indeed, Dick, carp fishing's most influential figure, often acknowledged the writings of B. B. as being an early stimulus. Until about 1960, the development of carp fishing tended to centre around specific fisheries and groups of anglers. These included Otto Overbeck and his friends at Croxby Pond around the turn of the century, the members of the Red Spinners Angling Society at Cheshunt Reservoir between 1911 and 1935, Albert Buckley and friends at Mapperley Reservoir between 1930 and 1947, members of the Becontree & District Angling Society fishing at Dagenham Lake between 1943 and 1964 and, of course, the Carp Catchers' Club members and their friends at Redmire Pool between 1951 and 1963.

In the early 1960s the appeal of carp fishing began to grow rapidly as a result of several different factors. The baby boom which followed World War II led, by the early 1960s, to large numbers of teenagers with new-found affluence and leisure. This coincided with a mushrooming of available carp fisheries, mainly the result of a vast increase in the number of sand and gravel pits created as a by-product of the post-war building boom. Not only did Dick Walker's weekly column in *Angling Times*, in the 1950s, inspire many to set about fishing for carp, it also encouraged those with influence to have carp stocked in the newly dug pits. The consequence of all this was that by the early 1960s there existed a young, open-minded generation of successful carp anglers. It was not long before some of them began writing about their experiences. Important contributions to the development of carp fishing were made during that decade by, among others, Roger Bowskill, Jim Gibbinson, Terry Eustace, Gerry Savage, Fred Wagstaffe, Bill Keal, Mike Winter, and, of course, Jack Hilton. Perhaps even more so in some ways than Dick Walker, it was Jack who popularized carp fishing. His writings seem to generate an enthusiasm that inspired so many to try to emulate his success.

Around this time the tackle trade started to wake up to the fact that a new market had sprung up. Specialist carp tackle began to appear, whereas previously much of it had been home-made. Some of it was not well conceived and was undoubtedly designed by people who did not fish for carp. The first mass-produced carp

Richard Walker, whose gifts as both angler and writer inspired so many others to take up carp fishing in the 1950s and 60s.

landing net proved so heavy it required two hands to wield it, which restricted carp fishing to a two-man operation. By the late 1960s, however, a range of carp products was available which, if not ideal in every case, certainly improved the chances of success.

Interest in carp fishing has grown steadily since the 'breakthrough' of Dick Walker and friends in the 1950s. Today there are many thousands of anglers who fish for carp. They range from dedicated specialists, who spend countless hours in pursuit of individual fish, to ordinary pleasure anglers who put a spare rod out in the hope of occasionally hooking a carp. This growth in carp fishing has seen a number of organizations established to cater for the interests of carp anglers. Generally, you get out of these organizations what you want. Subscriptions are about £8 per annum, and this entitles the member to three or four copies a year of extremely professional magazines dealing exclusively with carp. There are also conferences and meetings, some on a local level, instructional weekends, and discounts on tackle and fishing subscriptions. And of course, mem-

Landing a big Redmire carp at night. The large-mesh, knotted net used here has long been abandoned in favour of the knotless type.

bership provides the opportunity to meet other anglers with similar interests and ambitions. The main groups are:

The Carp Society, 33 Covert Road, Hainault, Ilford, Essex.
The Carp Anglers' Association, Castle Cary Press, Castle Cary, Somerset.
The British Carp Study Group, Cypryvan, Bedford Road, Lower Stondon, Bedfordshire.

HISTORIC BIG CARP

1793	18 lb (8 kg), Stourhead, Wiltshire
1836	22 lb (10 kg) netted, Mere at Pain's Hill, Surrey
1858	24 lb 8 oz (11 kg) netted, Great Pond, Harting, West Sussex
1872	22 lb (10 kg), Weston Park, Shropshire
1872	24 lb (11 kg), Great Pond, Harting, West Sussex
1881	21 lb 8 oz (10 kg), not known
1883	20 lb (9 kg), River Thames at Wallingford, Berkshire
1892	29 lb (13 kg) netted, Great Pond, Harting, West Sussex
1894	18 lb 1 oz (8 kg) G. Eady, Lake at Windsor, Berkshire
1899	23 lb 1 oz (10.5 kg) J. Holden, Broadwater Pond, Surrey
1902	17 lb 8 oz (8 kg) O. Overbeck, Croxby Pond, Lincolnshire
1903	29 lb (13 kg) found dead, Wytham Lake, Stamford, Lincolnshire
1907	19 lb 8 oz (9 kg) H. S. Locksmith, Weybridge Canal, Surrey
1907	20 lb (9 kg), Surrey pond
1911	22 lb 8 oz (10 kg) netted, Berkshire lake
1911	20 lb 8 oz (9.5 kg), Lake at Aldermaston, Berkshire
1912	26 lb 8 oz (12 kg) netted, Virginia Water, Surrey
1915	18 lb 5 oz (8.5 kg) O. J. Knudsen, Lake near Grantham, Lincolnshire
1916	20 lb 3 oz (9 kg) J. Andrews, Cheshunt Reservoir, Hertfordshire
1916	37 lb (17 kg) netted, Hampton Court, Greater London
1919	19 lb 8 oz (9 kg) J. T. Fisher, Warren Pond, Chingford, Essex
1920	18 lb 1 oz (8 kg) J. Crawley, River Adur, West Sussex
1921	24 lb (11 kg) netted, Birmingham reservoir
1922	26 lb (12 kg) found dead, Kent lake
1926	21 lb 10 oz (10 kg) A. E. Wyatt, Chingford, Essex

Note: SI (metric) weights are given to the nearest half kilogram.

Chris Yates with the fish that nearly knocked Dick Walker's Clarissa from her pedestal. Full of spawn, the fish was sadly soon to perish.

RECENT BIG CARP

Weight	Captor	Location
51 lb 8 oz (23·5 kg)	C. Yates	Redmire Pool, H. and Worcs 1980
45 lb 12 oz (21 kg)	R. MacDonald	Yateley, nr Camberley, Surrey 1984
44 lb 6 oz (20 kg)	R. Greenwood	Bedfordshire 1984
44 lb 4 oz (20 kg)	D. Baker	Yateley, nr Camberley, Surrey 1985
44 lb 4 oz (20 kg)	not known	Yateley, nr Camberley, Surrey 1984
44 lb (20 kg)	R. Walker	Redmire Pool, H. and Worcs 1952
43 lb 13½ oz (20 kg)	C. Yates	Redmire Pool, H. and Worcs 1972
43 lb 8 oz (19·5 kg)	K. O'Connor	Harrow, Greater London 1984
43 lb 4 oz (19·5 kg)	A. Tilbury	Yateley, nr Camberley, Surrey 1984
43 lb 4 oz (19·5 kg)	S. Fox	Yateley, nr Camberley, Surrey 1984
43 lb 4 oz (19·5 kg)	R. Fuller	Yateley, nr Camberley, Surrey 1987
43 lb 4 oz (19·5 kg)	C. Gibbins	Sandholme Pool, Humberside 1984
43 lb (19·5 kg)	G. Mountain	Trilakes, nr Camberley, Surrey 1983
42 lb 12 oz (19·5 kg)	M. Symonds	Waltham Abbey, Greater London 1976
42 lb (19 kg)	M. Lawson	Yateley, nr Camberley, Surrey 1989
42 lb (19 kg)	R. Clay	Billing Aquadrome, Northants 1966
42 lb (19 kg)	K. Hodder	Yateley, nr Camberley, Surrey 1979
42 lb (19 kg)	Z. Bojko	Harrow, Greater London 1984
41 lb 12 oz (19 kg)	R. Dix	Yateley, nr Camberley, Surrey 1985
41 lb 12 oz (19 kg)	D. Wibley	Staines, Greater London 1989
41 lb 10 oz (19 kg)	J. Wenczka	Yateley, nr Camberley, Surrey 1981
41 lb 8 oz (19 kg)	K. Nash	Essex 1985
41 lb 5 oz (18·5 kg)	C. Riddington	Yateley, nr Camberley, Surrey 1980
41 lb 4 oz (18·5 kg)	D. Wibley	Staines, Greater London 1988
40 lb 10 oz (18·5 kg)	J. Holt	Middlesex 1982
40 lb 8 oz (18·5 kg)	K. Clifford	Sandholme Pool, Humberside 1983
40 lb 8 oz (18·5 kg)	E. Price	Redmire Pool, H. and Worcs 1959
40 lb 8 oz (18·5 kg)	C. Swaden	Staines, Greater London 1980
40 lb 4 oz (18 kg)	K. Clifford	Sandholme Pool, Humberside 1984
40 lb 4 oz (18 kg)	L. Jackson	Harrow, Greater London 1983
40 lb 4 oz (18 kg)	R. Johnson	not known 1985
40 lb 3 oz (18 kg)	J. Hilton	Redmire Pool, H. and Worcs 1972
40 lb 3 oz (18 kg)	C. Swaden	Staines, Greater London 1980
40 lb ½ oz (18 kg)	R. Groombridge	Boxmoor 1966
40 lb (18 kg)	J. MacLeod	Redmire Pool, H. and Worcs 1972
40 lb (18 kg)	not known	East Peckham, Kent 1972
40 lb (18 kg)	A. Turner	not known
40 lb (18 kg)	P. Harper	Essex 1984

Note: SI (metric) weights are given to the nearest half kilogram.

CHAPTER TWO

THE NATURE OF THE CARP

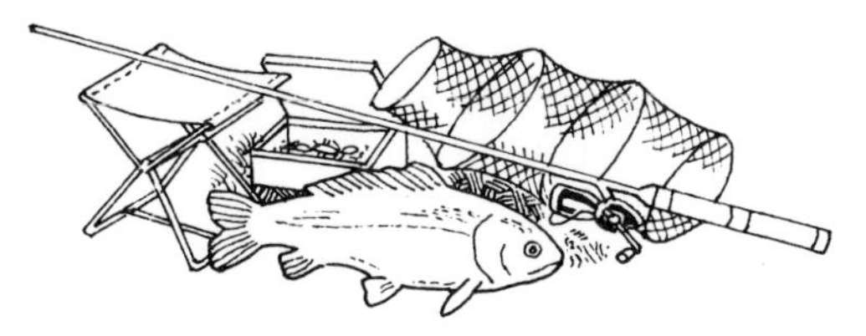

The ancestors of the carp, *Cyprinus carpio*, almost certainly originated in the area around the Caspian Sea at the end of the Pleistocene some 10,000 years ago. With the ending of the last Ice Age and the resulting higher temperatures the species colonized the Black Sea area, the Aral system, eastern Asia and, about 8000 years ago, the River Danube system. In about AD 15, a Roman camp was established near the mouth of the River Morava, a tributary of the Danube, and this later grew into a large town called Carnuntum, an important resting place on the much-used Amber Road.

The evidence suggests that it was from this area that carp were first transported throughout Europe. Having been transferred to Italy, and following the decline of the Roman Empire, the species' domestication continued, with the advent of Christianity, in monastery stewponds. It is likely that further stocks of carp from the Danube region were also later transferred to sites in Western Europe. With the establishment of monasteries, from the sixth century onwards, it became necessary for the monks to have a readily available source of fish to consume during their fasting periods, which covered more than a hundred days each year.

By the Middle Ages carp culture had become routine, not only in monasteries but also on private estates. And by 1600, when John Taverner wrote *Certain Experiments Concerning Fish and Fruite*, many of the practices of present-day fish culture were already well established in Britain. It is notable in Taverner's book that carp are given pride of place as a cultivated fish. However, by comparison with European countries, Britain has a very long coastline in relation to its area. Consequently, with the development in the early nineteenth century of surfaced roads, which allowed fast journeys to be made, sea fish could be carried considerable distances and still remain fresh. Then came ice, at first imported from Norway, which allowed the fish to be preserved. These developments caused the gradual demise of fish culture in general, and of that of the carp in particular, in Britain. However, in much of central and eastern Europe and Asia carp farming continues. In 1965 annual world production of carp was estimated at more than a million tons.

CHRONOLOGY OF THE CARP

AD 100– 400	The Romans introduce carp to the area west of the Danube.
500– 600	Further western introductions and rearing in ponds.
700–1300	Rearing on large scale in specially constructed ponds. Further introductions throughout Europe.
1400–1600	Large-scale culture and start of selective breeding. Introductions to Britain (early fifteenth century) and Ireland (early seventeenth century).
1700–	Intensification of breeding and cultivation. Introductions into the USA (1831), South Africa (1859), Australia (1860), and Canada (1880).

Two distinct forms of carp

In simple terms there are two clearly defined forms of carp: the pure wild carp and the selectively bred 'king' carp. The wild carp has a long, slender body, unlike the much deeper king carp, and lacks the hump between the top of the head and the back which is usually present in the domesticated forms. Breeding stocks of king carp, if left in isolation for a considerable time, often revert to a feral form of fully scaled carp, not dissimilar in appearance to the wild carp but

Hull-based specialist rod builder and tackle maker Bill Watson shows off a good-sized 'wildie' taken in the autumn.

generally possessing a hump. Not surprisingly, feral forms of the domesticated carp are often mistakenly identified as true wild carp.

The coloration of the 'wildie' is variable and is determined mainly by the environment. Usually, the top of the head and body are brownish-blue, the sides bright golden and the undersides off-white near the head, changing to a yellowish-orange near the tail. The dorsal fin has the same colour as the top of the body, as does the upper portion of the tail, while the lower part of the tail often has a reddish-orange tinge. The pectoral, ventral and anal fins can vary between slate grey and pale reddish-orange. Variations in colour in individual fish can take place throughout the year and are especially noticeable during spawning.

The fully scaled wild carp has greater strength and viability, including resistance to disease, than the domesticated carp. It has almost 20 per cent more red blood corpuscles and haemoglobin and its blood sugar level is 16–26 per cent higher. There is a far lower water content in its muscles and liver and a greater concentration of fat in its organs and glycogen in its liver. The vitamin A content in the 'wildie's' liver, eyes and intestines (the latter are considerably shorter than in the king carp) is also higher.

Strictly speaking, the wild carp has its origins in stocks introduced into Britain in the early fifteenth century and has very close biological similarities to the ancestral and modern Danubian wild carp. There are, at most, only a handful of waters in Britain which still contain true wild carp. Indeed, it is possible that they have already been lost forever, their purity impaired by interbreeding, at some stage, with carp with selectively bred characteristics. Perhaps true Danubian wild carp never even reached this country, for as early as the sixteenth century some selective breeding in Europe had already produced 'races' of carp, including those in which scales were few or absent, and which were biologically distinct from their predecessors.

It has been predicted that extinction is the probable eventual fate of the true wild carp. This would be a tragic loss to mankind. It has long been known that domestic cattle, when left to become wild, remain in poor condition, never attaining the quality of the strong, wild, ancestral auroch from which they are derived. It is similarly likely that feral carp will never achieve the condition and viability of

Volunteers rescuing several large carp to around 30 lb (14 kg), from an inhospitable gravel pit, before transferring them to another water.

the true wild carp. In cattle, scientifically directed selection would have a far better chance of improving production if genes of the extinct auroch were still available. When true wild carp have become extinct the same principle will almost certainly apply.

King carp

The term 'king' carp properly refers to the selectively bred races of carp evolved mainly in specific regions of Europe and primarily farmed for food. Some of the best known of these races are the Galician, Bohemian and Aischgrund. Two very important traits have been developed in king carp through selective breeding, the first of which is improved growth rates. Mass selection over many years has resulted in a carp which is thicker-set and has a faster growth rate and larger ultimate size than its wild ancestors. Naturally, an increased growth rate is a prime benefit to the fish farmer.

The second trait is variation in scale distribution. Selective breeding of naturally occurring mutants has resulted in four genetically distinct types of carp:

Dave Booth with a beautiful example of a fully-scaled mirror carp. Weighing 20 lb (9 kg), it was caught at Hemingford Grey, Cambridgeshire.

1 *The scaled carp* Fully scaled and similar in pattern to the wild carp. Sometimes known as the common carp.

2 *The scattered carp* Scales of differing sizes, randomly arranged in varying amounts on the body, principally characterized by a continuous row of scales along the back, from the head to the tail, and a group of scales near the head, with another group next to the tail. Along the lateral line, scales are either absent or, when they form a continuous row, are uneven and irregular. Often referred to as the mirror carp.

3 *The linear carp* Possesses a continuous, straight and quite regular row of scales along the lateral line. Occasionally there are further

This handsome fifteen-pounder (7 kg) caught by Malcolm Roberts from Fosshill Ponds has a scale pattern often mistaken for 'linear' scaling.

rows, one above and one below, usually incomplete. Also called the line carp.

4 *The nude carp* Scales are few and sometimes totally absent. If scales exist along the back they do not form a continuous row and are small. Often known as the leather carp.

Theoretically, the nude carp would be the preferred type for the food market as it requires little or no scaling. However, the principal genes which determine the scale patterns also affect other biological characteristics. Consequently, the linear and nude carp both show reduced viability and lower growth rates, in addition to other detrimental characteristics, when compared with the fully scaled and scattered carp. For this reason the scattered carp is almost always the type produced in European fish farms.

Variable coloration

The coloration of the king carp is very variable. Apart from the environmental influences, a number of mutant forms of pigmentation have been identified, having been selectively bred into several races. Various blue mutations occur in domesticated carp in Germany, Israel and Poland. Gold, red and orange mutants, all with black eyes, can be found in many countries both in the domesticated races and in wild populations. There are also records of grey, yellow, silver, green, white, violet, brown and albino varieties of carp. It is assumed that most of these variants depend on one, sometimes two or three, genes affecting the development of pigment cells. Many of these mutations have been used in the breeding of ornamental carp, particularly in Japan. The cultivation of koi carp in that country has a long history, and is said to date from around AD 1000.

What exists, in the natural waters of Britain, is a kaleidoscope of carp types ranging from possibly true 'wildies' to various pure races of king carp, but mostly a mishmash of all sorts.

CHAPTER THREE

THE CARP'S HABITS AND ENVIRONMENT

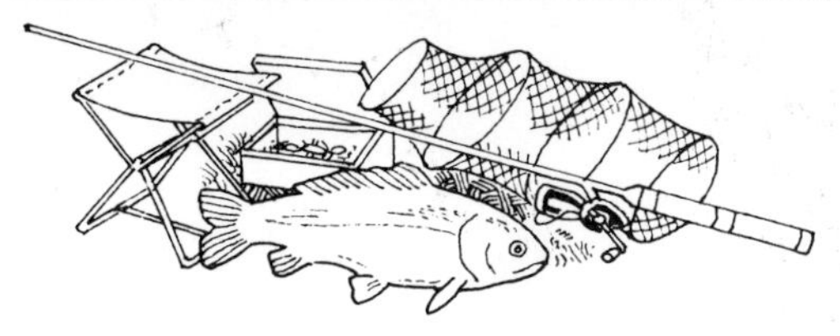

A highly adaptable fish, the carp is able to survive an extreme range of environmental conditions. Its robust nature has allowed the carp to establish itself in waters ranging from stagnant, overgrown, semi-polluted farm ponds, to fast-flowing chalk streams. There is no other species of freshwater fish which can exist in such a diverse range of environments. The carp is now widely distributed, with breeding populations in Europe, the Soviet Union, China, America, Canada, Australia and the Far East.

The species has a natural preference for warm water. Margaret Varley states in her book *British Freshwater Fishes* that experiments in temperature gradients showed that after acclimatization carp preferred a water temperature of 32 °C (90 °F). However, other evidence suggests that this figure is too high. Certainly, experiments carried out by Dr David Brown for the CEGB at Radcliffe-on-Soar Power Station and also the practical experience of carp farmers such as Ken Ryder of Humberside Fisheries indicate that, when other factors remain constant, carp show increased growth with temperature increase up to a limit of about 27 °C (81 °F). Above this temperature growth becomes erratic and finally ceases. It would seem strange, therefore, that a fish would prefer a water temperature where, at the very least, its growth is severely inhibited. I believe that the optimum temperature for carp is about 25–27 °C (77–81 °F). These water temperatures are not normally achieved in Britain; indeed the mean air temperature for the hottest month of the year, in the south, is around 16–18 °C (61–64 °F). It is reasonable to assume, then, that in Britain carp do not achieve their maximum

A fine leather carp caught by the author at Redmire. The signs of a week-long session are showing, but a fish like this makes it worthwhile.

potential size. This supposition is borne out by the facts. Very few British carp reach a maximum weight of over 40 lb (18 kg). Only a handful of different fish heavier than this have ever been caught, and of these the majority came from southern England. In other parts of the world, such as Spain, the South of France, and South Africa, where water temperatures are higher throughout the year, many carp of over 50 lb (23 kg) and up to a maximum of about 80 lb (36 kg) have been reported. It would seem likely that the greatest weight a carp can grow to is about 80–100 lb (36–45 kg).

Although carp will survive in a wide range of ponds, lakes, rivers and canals, there are specific requirements for spawning success and good growth. The latter is dependent upon two main environmental factors, water temperature and available food, but others, such as oxygen levels, disturbance and disease, also play their part. Although shallow water warms up quickly, it also cools down quickly, so an ideal fishery would have both shallows and some relatively deep water. Food production begins with sunlight, and since light penetration in water rarely exceeds 20 ft (6 m), depths greater than this produce little food. Coloured water also cuts down sunlight, so, in general, clear ponds, lakes and gravel pits where most of the water is shallower than 15 ft (4.5 m) and there is a variety of luxuriant submerged plant life, are best suited to the growth of carp. Aquatic plant life is important for many reasons. It has some direct food value but, more importantly, it is the key to the more advanced food items which make up the main source of the carp's natural diet. Plant life also provides oxygen through photosynthesis. In her excellent book *Better Angling with Simple Science*, Mary Pratt explains concisely the important role played by aquatic plants: 'Green plants are thus the food factories of the living world; they are solar energy traps "par excellence", collecting the sun's radiant energy and storing it up in complex foodstuffs of their own making, to be used by themselves, or, in time, by other organisms which feed on plants. They also do the important job of refurbishing supplies of oxygen. The Biblical saying "All flesh is grass" has been quoted many times by biologists trying to emphasize the all-important function of photosynthesis.' Aquatic plant life is therefore a good indicator of the productivity of a fishery. Those rivers, canals and still waters which have a varied and prolific weed growth tend to be the fisheries with the biggest fish.

Chemical composition

Another factor with an important bearing on food production is the amount and type of dissolved chemicals present. These normally derive from the naturally occurring minerals in the land around the fishery, but sometimes come from other sources, such as agricultural fertilizers and sewage farms. However, in too great a quantity, sewage effluent, agricultural fertilizers and even some natural minerals can cause problems. Large amounts of sewage effluent are simply poisonous to fish and even when they do not act as a direct poison their high organic content can often lead to de-oxygenation.

In small quantities, sewage can make fisheries more productive. A good example is a chain of well known and productive gravel pits near, and in some cases connected to, the River Colne, in West London, which accepts the treated effluent from a number of sewage works. A similar situation exists at the famous Yateley gravel pits, on the Surrey/Hampshire border, where the sewage-enriched River Blackwater runs close enough to the lakes to permeate the gravel strata. The enrichment of rivers and still-waters by the leaching of organic and inorganic agricultural fertilizers has been increasing gradually since the end of World War II. Again, where the quantities are small, this can have beneficial results on fisheries, but where the additions are excessive or prolonged, it can result in dense algal blooms which can also cause de-oxygenation.

The pH value

Water can be acidic, neutral or alkaline and the measure of this is the 'pH value'. A pH value of 7 denotes neutral water, lower than 7 is acid, and higher than 7 is alkaline. Most natural waters have a pH of between 5.5 and 10. Acid water is normally less productive than alkaline water, as it is usually lacking in some important chemicals, particularly calcium carbonate. These are essential for the proliferation of many plants and aquatic insects which form the food of fish. Generally, waters with a pH value of between 7.5 and 9.0 make the most productive carp fisheries.

While still-waters generally provide the best conditions for carp, the species also thrives in some canals and rivers. Probably the best example is the River Trent, certain areas of which offer very good carp fishing, even in winter. The River Nene once had an excellent reputation for very large carp in the stretch around Peterborough and wild carp in its upper reaches, but sadly the river is not so prolific nowadays. The Great Ouse has also produced some very large carp in the past, fish of over 30 lb (14 kg) coming from the St Neots power station warm-water outfall. The Thames has held good stocks of carp since the beginning of this century, and nowadays, like the Trent, offers excellent carp sport, with big fish present in many stretches. The Royal Military Canal, in Kent, has a long-standing reputation for large carp to over 30 lb (14 kg) and others, like the Grand Union Canal, hold good stocks of smaller carp.

Regular maintenance work such as this at Cave Castle, Yorkshire, carp syndicate is an indispensable part of the club and syndicate scene.

The productivity of a fishery can be measured in the total weight of fish it sustains. A rich water will support as much as 1000 lb per acre (1120 kg/hectare) but that could comprise fifty carp of 20 lb (9 kg) each or 1000 carp weighing 1 lb (0.5 kg) each. Therefore rich, productive fisheries do not always contain big fish. These are usually present in such fisheries where there is a low number of fish. This situation ensures ample food supplies, allowing the fish to grow without competition. Low fish densities are usually related to poor recruitment or high predation.

There is a widely held, but erroneous, belief that carp do not often spawn successfully in Britain. This misunderstanding has come about because it is unusual to find fisheries with abundant stocks of carp which have not been artificially introduced. The fact is that while carp have no difficulty in spawning even in the far north, the eggs produced are particularly sensitive to low temperatures. Furthermore, because of the short period between spawning and the onset of winter (June/July–October), the fry do not usually manage to store enough fat reserves to allow them to survive their first winter. Textbooks and the experience of carp farms suggest that at temperatures below 8 °C (46 °F) carp feed very little and that they cease feeding altogether at about 5 °C (41 °F). In experiments I carried out in tanks holding several hundred small carp, at 8 °C (46 °F) all the carp were seen to feed after not being fed for several hours. At 10 °C (50 °F) feeding became aggressive. At 5 °C (41 °F) about 20 per cent of the fish still fed and the lowest observed feeding temperature, for a handful of fish, was 2 °C (36 °F).

Mature carp–males at least three to four years old and females at least four to five years old–spawn between the end of May and mid-July, when the combination of water temperature and day length is optimal. In the last stages of this development there will be chemosensory interaction between the male and female fish, with the release of chemical stimuli. The eggs are usually 10–30 per cent of the total body weight of the female just before spawning. A 10 lb (4.5 kg) female carp would release around one million eggs which are about 1 mm in diameter and swell to about 1.6 mm after contact with water. They are slightly opaque and sticky, and after being shed become attached to water plants or fine fibrous tree roots.

Spawning usually takes place in shallow water but, particularly if no shallow water exists, carp will spawn at the surface, above submerged aquatic vegetation over deep water. The eggs hatch in about three to five days, depending on water temperature. The fry, which are about 5 mm in length, have a yolk-sac which is absorbed over the first few days as they begin to feed on rotifers and small crustaceans, mainly water fleas. By the end of the summer the young carp are prepared to feed on a much wider variety of food items, including the larvae and pupae of chironomids, water beetles, small snails and various crustaceans. As they grow, they feed on a very wide range of naturally occurring animal and vegetable materials.

It has been suggested that, because carp do not possess in their gut the necessary bacterial fauna to break down the cellulose wall material both for its own nutritive value (small as that may be), and to make the contents of the plant cells available, they do not derive any nutritional value from plant life. While it is certainly true that carp derive little benefit from the cellulose itself, their very efficient pharyngeal teeth can break down the plant walls, giving access to the digestible cell interiors. It is likely that even herbivores, such as the grass carp, *Ctenopharyngodon idellus*, rely heavily on this mechanical breakdown of plant cell walls and much, chemically unaltered, cell wall is excreted. At times carp can exhibit very deliberate and selective feeding habits. They have been known to feed on other fish and I have seen them feeding on shoals of tadpoles. Scientific research (Stein, Kitchell and Knezevic, 1974) has clearly shown that carp can feed selectively on one specific species of mollusc from a range of molluscs of equal availability. There appeared to be beneficial reasons for this selective feeding.

The carp's senses

The adult carp has often been described as a bottom-feeding fish, and it is true that much of its time is spent slowly grazing in close contact with the bottom, relying on sight, smell and taste. However, the experience of anglers confirms that carp will readily feed in mid-water and on the surface.

In carp, taste is primarily related to food finding and feeding, whereas smell, which likewise has an important role in food location, has further uses in reproduction and social behaviour. Smell sensors are found inside the nostrils of the carp and respond when water containing either natural or artificial stimuli passes through. Only substances which are soluble in water can therefore be detected in this way. The smell sensors in fish are extremely sensitive, much more so than those of humans. (The eel, whose ability in this area compares favourably with that of the dog, can detect certain chemicals when they are present in water at a concentration lower than one part in a million billion.) The initial response to food is, therefore, usually brought about by smell and this can take place at considerable distances. The functions of taste and sight are used in much closer proximity to food. The taste receptors, resembling taste buds in mammals, are situated on the carp's barbels, on the gill rakers, on the body and around the mouth, particularly in the roof of the mouth. Those situated in the roof of the mouth appear to be the most important.

Carp Society founder member Greg Fletcher with a mirror carp of a size commonly caught. It was taken from Tilery Lake, Humberside.

Sight in fish assists in the capture of food, finding shelter, avoiding predators, and orientation. Yet many species, particularly carp, appear to have no difficulty in surviving, indeed flourishing, in the wild when blind. Carp have two types of optic cell: rods and cones. The rods are very sensitive to light, but can only distinguish objects in tones of grey. By contrast, the cones are of little use in very low light conditions but they do provide colour vision when good light is available. Their ability to distinguish between different colours is approximately equivalent to that of humans, and indeed there is evidence that they may surpass human capability by coping with the violet end of the spectrum.

However, colour is nothing more than the quantity of light reflected from the surface of an object. The deeper an object is in water, the more the constituent shades of red, yellow and green disappear. A red object is only red for as long as the light falling on it contains the red part of the spectrum and just a few metres under water much of the red-yellow component of light disappears. At greater depths only the blue component remains. In a fish the lens is situated close to the front of the eye, and protrudes through the pupil, so ensuring a wide field of vision. The field of vision for each eye is about 160° horizontally and about 150° vertically. Directly in front of the fish a field of vision of about 20° is covered by both eyes simultaneously. Fish see with the sharpest vision at the front, while their side vision is somewhat blurred.

Acute hearing

Carp have particularly good hearing. Like most fish they possess two internal ears, called labyrinths, which are situated on either side of the brain. Part of each labyrinth is concerned with the balance and orientation of the fish, and the other parts, called otoliths, are used for hearing. The acute hearing of the carp is due to the swim-bladder being connected to the ears by a series of bones known as the Weberian ossicles. These are responsible for transmitting the vibrations received by the swim-bladder (which acts as an additional aid to hearing) to the inner ear. Fish can often hear sound and vibration caused by bankside activity. There is little doubt that, on most fisheries, carp have come to associate such sounds with danger. One example of this made a great impression on me. I was watching, from the branches of a tree, several carp feeding in Redmire Pool's shallows. A few quiet words to a friend who was concealed below in the undergrowth sent the carp powering off in panic towards deep water. When I see young carp anglers hammering their umbrella poles into the ground with a large mallet, I wonder just how many frightened carp are similarly disappearing.

The least understood of all the senses of fish is the lateral line. This is a series of sense organs in the form of small, open tubes penetrating the scales, or skin, and connected by a canal filled with mucus. Vibration and water movements are detected by fine, hair-like cupulae in the bottom of the canal, which cause impulses to be sent to the brain. The lateral line can be seen as an additional way of telling the fish what is going on around it, but it also provides a highly effective sense of distance. Even blind fish constantly receive a 'picture' of their immediate surroundings.

Len Arbery with a superb 24 lb (10.8 kg) common, the sort of carp many anglers still dream of catching.

Top A specimen mirror carp weighing 22 lb (9.9 kg).

Above A corner of a typical carp lake. The vegetation includes water-lilies, rushes, reeds and overhanging willows.

Clive Gibbins with a fine brace of big carp caught from a Hull & District water.

Kevin Clifford with an early morning brace of carp caught on Richworth boilies, flavoured with Salmon Supreme.

CHAPTER FOUR

TACKLE

For as long as man has hunted fish for food he has used fishing tackle. Stones and crude spears may have formed his first armoury, but human ingenuity was soon searching for other ways to catch fish. Consequently, the development of gorges, lines, hooks, rods, and then reels, took place. We do not know precisely when man first became interested in angling as a sport, rather than as a means of securing food, but it was long ago. The distinction is amply demonstrated in two Egyptian drawings. The first, dating from about 2000 BC, shows a man who is obviously poor, probably a slave, fishing for food. The second, from around 1400 BC, depicts a gentleman of leisure enjoying a bit of fishing. His clothes and general demeanour show that pleasure must be the objective since he is obviously wealthy enough to buy fish or pay others to catch them. The evolution of fishing for sport required the development of tackle and methods which give pleasure rather than simply provide the means to procure food.

MODERN CARP TACKLE BY LEN ARBERY

It is extremely difficult for anyone who has been carp fishing for only a few years to realize how radically specialized tackle has changed. Twenty years ago there were a few rods designed with carp in mind, but precious little else in the way of purpose-made carp tackle. Most items had to be modified or home made – or you went without! Richard Walker did more than anyone to rectify this situation, by designing and making sound carp tackle and then demonstrating that it worked successfully. However, the tackle trade, as a whole, was slow to catch on.

To be fair, the major tackle manufacturers could not justify the costs of design and development at a time when the potential market was so tiny. It was left to the smaller, progressive tackle businesses to fill the gap. People like B. James & Son, of Ealing, West London, who produced the first proprietary carp landing net. This was based on a design by Dick Walker, as was the first commercially successful electric bite alarm, 'The Heron', which was put on the market by Jack Opie. It amuses me now to listen to a tiny sub-culture of carp anglers who recommend the use of old-fashioned tackle, proclaiming it to be as good, and as efficient, as its modern counterparts. The best of modern tackle is far superior in every way. It is funny to see these chaps running around extolling the virtues of Richard Walker Mark IV split-cane carp rods, when Dick himself would not have anything to do with them and preferred carbon-fibre! Nostalgia is all very well, but the place for antique tackle is in the fishing den, not on the banks of a carp pool.

Take it from me, who had no choice at one time but to suffer with inferior tackle: more fish are lost as a result of it than are landed. I do not hear many of these anglers who laud old tackle say much about the hooks we had to endure in the early days, which is just as well as, almost without exception, they were quite dreadful. I clearly remember talking at a London tackle show to a representative of a hook manufacturer who boasted that his company produced some 5000 different hook patterns. When I pointed out that not one of them was suitable for carp fishing he stomped off in a huff, mumbling about some people never being satisfied. Nowadays, by contrast, we have people at the hookmakers, like Alan Bramley of Partridge, who are always willing to listen to new ideas and hear about the problems of the specialist angler. It is this welcome change of attitude that has been responsible for the overall excellent quality and wide variety of carp tackle available today.

A word of warning: an item of tackle that suits me, may not suit you. It still causes me acute discomfort to recollect what happened when the first pre-stretched monofilament line, Platil Stark, was introduced. My friends, including two of the very best carp anglers of all time – Bill Quinlan and Jack Hilton – recommended that 'Stark' was the best development since glass-fibre rods and used it exclusively. However, after many unexplained breakages and lost fish, I just had to accept that it did not work for me.

RODS

The modern carbon-fibre carp rod, like those made of boron, Kevlar and various composites, casts further and more accurately, picks up line quicker, and is essentially stronger, lighter and more durable than anything that has preceded it. The adaptability of this material however, does not guarantee that one single design will answer all situations and circumstances. As yet, I have not fished vast tracts of water with great depths, where a 13 ft (395 cm), 3 lb (1.35 kg) test-curve rod would prove an advantage. My everyday 'workhorses' are based on Sportex blanks and are 11 ft (335 cm) long with a test curve of 2¼ lb (1 kg). This type of rod is fine for many of the normal carp-fishing situations. Fuji reel seats and rod rings are used throughout. These rods were made for me by the Kent rod builder Bruce Ashby, himself a noted carp catcher, and have completed several seasons' hard work without trouble. The rings, however, are to be replaced with a type incorporating the latest developments. The new rings are supplied by Ryobi Masterline and, being the world's first rings made from carbon-fibre, are a technological breakthrough. They are called 'Ferox Flo-Lite' and are moulded from a flexible polymer mix which is light and, more importantly, causes minimal interference with the action of the rod. They also have virtually wearproof ceramic linings and are both shockproof and tough. Furthermore, the neatly tapering feet make for easy whipping, so a professional finish can be readily achieved.

Carp rods at a sensible price

Not long ago it was fair to say that there was no such thing as a good, reasonably priced carp rod. Happily, nowadays the situation is different. Recently I have been testing an 11 ft (335 cm) carp rod made of boron by Silstar. This, the 3574–330 model, is a superb rod where a soft, progressive action is required. As purchased, it has big clumsy rings and I personally do not like the large-diameter handle. However, neither of these criticisms prevents the rod catching fish. With these Silstar rods, lines up to 8 lb (3.5 kg) breaking strain are readily managed and I dare say, in desperate circumstances, it would be possible to use even heavier lines. These rods are the most versatile I have so far come across.

A well-balanced set-up: 11-ft (335-cm) Armalite rods, Shimano 3500 reels and Optonic bite alarms.

Other carp rods I keep hearing good remarks about include the 'Cougar' range by Graham Phillips. These are coloured light grey, light in weight (5¾ oz/16 g) for a 2 lb (0.9 kg) test-curve, 12 ft (365 cm) model, and have the latest high-performance Fuji rings. Another good range are the 'Armalites' by Century Composites. These are very popular rods even though rather expensive. They are made in lengths between 11 ft (335 cm) and 13 ft (395 cm), and have test curves between 1½ lb (0.7 kg) and 3 lb (1.35 kg), a range which should cover almost every situation, from precision margin fishing to the most demanding long-distance casting.

The lead from an ordinary pencil, when applied to the spigot of a carbon-fibre rod, will prevent the joint jamming.

REELS

It is my belief that only reels of the fixed-spool type are worth considering for carp fishing. At various times centrepins and multipliers have been used, but both suffer from considerable drawbacks.

The days when *all* big-fish men relied on Mitchell reels are long gone. Although the competitors have caught up, the Mitchell reel was, and still is overall, an excellent piece of workmanship. The line-laying system and the width of the spool on the popular 300 and 410 models have not yet been equalled, but the inadequate line roller in the bale-arm, and the indecisive return of the bale-arm itself, together with a clutch that needs constant adjustment, have led many British carp anglers to try other manufacturers' models. The bale-arm problems can be partly remedied by using a stronger spring. These, following complaints by carp anglers, have been made available by the makers (Part No 30224C).

Superb engineering was the hallmark of ABU's early 'Cardinal' 55 and 57 models. Their bale-arm return and roller, and the clutch, were absolutely first-class. I would still be using mine today if another reel, with a unique feature, had not been introduced – the Shimano 'Baitrunner'. In some styles of fishing the 'baitrunner' feature is an absolute boon in that it allows a fish to take line without your leaving the bale-arm open. Pushing a special lever forward disengages the gearing, providing a free-running line. This can be tensioned, adjustments being made for undertow, drifting weed, or the current. The gearing is engaged as soon as the handle is turned forward.

There are several different 'Baitrunner' models made by Shimano. I use the BTR 3500, which suffices for the majority of situations, but where extremely long distances have to be achieved, the BTR 4500 is more suitable. At the time of writing, these reels have performed reliably for two seasons. I have only two small criticisms: the reel should be of the 'push-on' type, and the reverse lever is fiddly to operate as it is tucked away right under the reel.

LINES AND HOOKS

A skilful angler can manage with questionable rods and reels. He would, however, be just as unsuccessful as the most incompetent angler if he used poor-quality hooks and lines. It is absolutely essential that the very best hooks and lines obtainable are used if consistent success is to be enjoyed.

Of the many monofilament lines now available, my choice for the

Far from the madding crowd. An easy-going style of carp fishing can be just as successful as the 'three rods and a bivvy' approach.

majority of situations is Maxima. This brand has good knot strength, is easy to handle, reasonably resistant to abrasion, has a consistent and fine diameter for its breaking strain and an unobtrusive colour. But, above all else, I find it very reliable. Its one failing is that it is a fairly springy line, and, because of this, problems are experienced in breaking strains of over 8–10 lb (3.5–4.5 kg). Sylcast is another excellent choice, and is used by many carp anglers. It is considerably more resistant to abrasion than Maxima, and therefore probably more suitable to gravel-pit fishing. It is also cheaper.

There are already many lines to choose from, with new ones being introduced fairly regularly, and there will undoubtedly be some major developments soon, with substantial improvements. I have recently been trying Bayer's 'Ultima' and found it particularly limp for its diameter. But other excellent monofilaments arc Trilene, Racine and Brent, the latter being both cheap and reliable.

Fishing with fine line

When it is essential to use the finest line available, my first choice would be Drennan 'Double Strength'. It must be remembered that, as with all small-diameter and pre-stretched line, the slightest damage will seriously affect its strength. These types of line also seem susceptible to sudden shock, so it is important to be constantly alert to any line damage and to employ rods with a softish action.

Sometimes it is necessary, particularly with certain rigs, to use a braided line. Because braided line has a large diameter for its breaking strain, it is generally unsuitable for use on the reel, and is therefore used mainly for hook links. The reason it is used at all is its limpness when compared to monofil. The Berkeley company supply a very reliable braided Dacron line called 'Premium Braid', which is supplied on 50 yard (46 m) spools of 10 lb (4.5 kg) and 12 lb (5.5 kg) breaking strain. It has good knot and wet strength, and it is important to remember that many braided lines lose a lot of their strength when wet. One make I recently tested, which was rated at 10 lb (4.5 kg) breaking strain, broke at less than 7 lb (3 kg) when knotted and after being immersed in water for an hour.

The search for even more supple hook-link materials has resulted in the use of such things as waxed dental floss, which is obtainable from any chemist. The breaking strain depends on which brand is purchased, but most seems to be 6–10 lb (2.7–4.5 kg). A recent development has been the availability of Kryston 'Multi-Strand'. This hook-link material consists of hundreds of high-tensile-strength micro-diameter fibres and in its normal state has a breaking strain of about 70 lb (32 kg). It can, however, be split down to obtain the required strength for any situation. Kryston has good knot strength and is very resistant to abrasion, but does require very careful use. It certainly appears to offer some advantages on waters where the carp have 'seen it all before'.

Over the last few years the choice of hooks has improved considerably. There now are available first-class hooks to suit every conceivable set of circumstances. Kamatsu hooks were the first of the 'high-tech' patterns I encountered. Their chemically contrived sharpness soon became renowned among the big-fish fraternity and everyone seemed to be using them. Nowadays their trade name is Kamasan, but, though the name has changed, the quality remains first-class. These hooks come in well designed boxes which, unlike some others, do not fall apart. Each box contains fifty hooks, and the pattern I invariably use is B980.

We have come to expect superb tackle from Peter Drennan, and his hooks are no exception. I use several of his patterns, including the 'Carbon Specimen' and the 'Super Specialist'. Both types are made from high-carbon steel wire, are forged, and have chemically sharpened points.

Improved hooking power

In 1985 Kevin Maddocks sent me a pre-production sample of his 'hair-rig' hooks to field-test. The surprising feature of this pattern is that the point is turned *away* from the shank, a design that is known as 'outpoint'. The idea behind this feature is that a fish trying to eject the hook is more likely to prick itself than on a hook with the point parallel to the shank. The points on the initial batch of the Maddocks 211 hooks were not sharp enough and it proved virtually impossible to improve them with a stone. Now they are available in the tackle shops, and Partridge, the manufacturers, have got an excellent point on them by chemical means. Partridge have recently produced an even stronger version, the GRS 1321 – Kevin Maddocks's Cassien Carp Hook – designed for fishing near snags for the huge carp of St Cassien in the South of France.

There are other reliable hooks available, among which are Partridge's 'Jack Hilton Carp Hooks', Mustad's 34021 and several models from Au Lion D'Or, including spade-end hooks with the pattern numbers 1535 and 1540, which are both very strong. A spade-end hook weighs slightly less than its eyed counterpart, which may be important with the current rigs and a small bait.

Barbless hooks are a liability in carp fishing. Any fish which becomes temporarily snagged or weeded-up will immediately get rid of one. A hook with a small barb will also be ultimately shed, but it will at least offer a little time in which the carp, if great care is used, may be extracted.

Need it be stressed yet again how important it is to test each and every hook before use? Odd faulty hooks, or even batches, can slip through the manufacturer's quality control, and if you do not check your hooks it always seems to be the case that the faulty hook is on the end of your line at the same time as that huge carp.

LANDING NETS

There is one item of carp tackle that still is not readily available over the shop counter: an efficient, lightweight, but robust landing net of suitable dimensions. Of course, there are a number of carp landing nets sold, but I have not yet seen one which completely satisfies me. Consequently I continue to use the type I designed (with the help of Bill Quinlan and Roger Smith) and made myself in 1968. As far as I am aware, it was the first time *hollow* glass-fibre had been used for a landing net. My net has had later additions such as a soft micro-mesh purse, but it has never broken or let me down. Over the years I have been persuaded to make these landing nets for various friends, and in all that time I have only ever had two brought back for repair. One angler stood on his and the other drove over it in his car! Of the types I have seen, those produced by Alan Brown of Hitchin and Terry Eustace of Birmingham, provide good value for money.

Ideal size for landing nets

The actual net itself should not be too deep, certainly no more than 3 ft (90 cm), otherwise it will be difficult to lift the carp clear of bankside vegetation, bushes and steep banking and the risk of damaging the fish will be increased. The material must be knotless – indeed, knotted nets are illegal in many Water Authority areas – and the bottom of the net should be made of very soft micro-mesh to cushion the fish when it is lifted.

Finally, let me clear up a misconception regarding the design of landing nets. Triangular nets are no less efficient than round ones, despite what has been written in some quarters. Nor do the corners of triangular nets get caught in the weed.

ROD RESTS

Rod rests are arguably the most abused items of tackle so, without being too heavy or bulky, they need to be made of the sturdiest material. Stainless steel is definitely best, but is difficult to machine, and so components made from it are not cheap. On the other hand, stainless-steel is virtually indestructible, so that tackle made of it should last a lifetime, proving very economical.

Two pairs of extending rod rests, each pair of differing length, will suffice for all but exceptional circumstances. The shorter of mine are 17 in (43 cm) long when closed and 32 in (80 cm) fully extended and are constructed from ⅜ in (1 cm) diameter tube. The dimensions of the longer pair vary between 30 in (75 cm) and 50 in (125 cm) and are made from ½ in (1.25 cm) diameter tube. Both have solid, stainless-steel rod centres which are also pointed, so that if required they can be used independently, for greater versatility. Buzzer bars can be screwed into both the front and rear rests of each pair. Usually the front buzzer bar holds the bite alarms and there are non-slip butt rests at the rear.

Excellent stainless-steel rod rests of the type described are marketed by Gardner, Kevin Nash, Rod Hutchinson, Penge Tackle and the Middlesex Angling Centre.

On some waters it can be the devil's own job to get rod rests (and brolly poles) into the ground. Certain banks, including gravel pits and concrete-sided reservoirs, can be impossible. The answer is the Gardner 'Rod-Pod', designed and marketed for just this situation. It consists of square tubing with adjustable legs. At each end clamps hold a standard rod rest which is inserted so as to touch the ground. The 'Rod-Pod' offers excellent support and, as it is reasonably light, the whole set-up can be moved from one area to another without being dismantled.

BUZZERS

The vast majority of carp anglers use the Optonic bite indicator, manufactured by Dellareed Ltd. The original concept was brilliant, although the earlier models had several shortcomings. My own and many other carp anglers' Optonic heads were 'modified' by Les Bamford before Dellareed took legal action to stop the practice.

This embargo has made the heads modified by Les, and by Delkim, much sought after. If you want to get hold of a pair, you will have to scour the advertisements for secondhand tackle and be prepared to spend a lot.

Optional extras

The present Dellareed models are now similar in many respects to those that have been customized. They are known as the 'Super' and the 'Special Compact'. It is advisable to obtain a couple of additional items to complement the Optonic system. The 'v' in which the rod is located on the Optonic is of a shallow angle and so in strong winds the rod is easily dislodged. A fast-taking fish can bring about the same result. A pair of 'ears' will solve this problem. Dellareed supply them, but with a minimum of DIY ability it is easy enough to make them. The screw thread, by which the Optonic is attached to the buzzer bar, is not very durable. An alternative made from diecast alloy, is much more satisfactory and is marketed under the trade name 'Opti-polo' and distributed by Kevin Nash Tackle.

Until recently, the best batteries for buzzers were undoubtedly those made by Duracell. Now, however, this supremacy is threatened. Kodak, the photographic manufacturers, have entered the market with high-performance batteries with a consistently long life, as well as extended shelf life. This last feature is particularly important to carp anglers, because the last thing you need when fishing miles from anywhere, in the pouring rain in the middle of the night, is spare batteries that have gone flat. For use in the Optonic the Kodak Ultralife U9VL battery is recommended. This battery is of the very latest design and is the first to use a lithium cell. It has about double the life expectancy of current high-performance batteries and up to ten times the life of an ordinary zinc-carbon battery. Its shelf life is claimed to be up to ten years.

SPRING BALANCES

For your own peace of mind the spring balance on which you weigh your catches should be accurate, reliable and easy to read. The familiar Avon dial balances come well recommended but I do not use them. Though reasonably accurate and reliable, the Avon model suitable for heavy fish such as carp can cause confusion. The pointer makes more than one revolution round the dial and a colour change, seen through a separate aperture, signifies this. Many mistakes have been made, and not all of them by inexperienced anglers. My own balances are by Salter and are made from tubular brass. They are quite expensive but, with regular maintenance and care, should last a lifetime. Every close season I have them checked at the local Weights and Measures Centre for accuracy. The cost for this service is very reasonable. For optimists, and Cassien freaks, Kevin Nash Tackle and Reuben Heaton distribute dial scales of much greater capacity.

SUNDRIES

To prevent injury to carp on the bank, it is important to gently lay the fish on something soft. Deep grass is all right but, particularly on gravel pits, suitable areas are not always available. Therefore I always carry a 3x2 ft (75x60 cm) piece of carpet underlay – the stuff that is about ½ in (1.25 cm) thick and made of dimpled foam rubber. This is ideal and can be rolled around the base of the rod holdall, and secured with a piece of string. Purpose-made unhooking mats are available and because they are waterproof they do not absorb water or fish slime. ET Products and Kevin Nash Tackle both produce good-quality mats.

A variety of weigh slings are available, the majority well made. They are very simple to make, particularly if you can enlist the help of someone handy with a needle and thread. A piece of heavy-duty net curtain and a sowing machine are all that are really needed. The best material to use for the stitching is nylon monofilament of about 2 lb (0.9 kg) breaking strain, which is virtually rot-proof.

Catapults

These are an essential addition to the carp angler's kit. My armoury contains three types. The first is from the Peter Drennan range and is specifically designed for maggots. I find it ideal for small particle baits and 'mini-boilies'. The second is a 'Black Widow' and is used for firing 'boilies' out to medium range. The third is the Barnett 'Diablo', which is reserved for extreme distances. In capable hands a

Veteran angling writer Fred J. Taylor using a catapult to fire out free offerings of sweetcorn on a Yorkshire carp water.

throwing stick is so much quicker than a catapult and can be very accurate. However, throwing sticks are very tiring on the arm and should be used only where really necessary, since they can, in the long-term, cause joint problems or even arthritis.

Some people, particularly club officials, frown upon the use of bivouacs, and when they are used for protracted stays at the waterside I can understand the objection. Nevertheless, if a weekend's sortie is planned, a 'bivvy' will make the stay so much more comfortable. During bad weather they can make the difference between catching and not catching, because nothing saps an angler's confidence more than being wet and cold and constantly worrying about how to keep the rain out! The alternative to a bivouac is storm-sides. To get the best from these some modification is usually necessary. Velcro tape stitched to both the storm-sides and the edge of the umbrella will ensure a secure and weatherproof seal. They can be left in place, folding inside the brolly when not needed.

The larger umbrellas are best. They provide enough space, in bad weather, for a bed-chair, the storage of fishing equipment and food, and room to cook. The Steadfast company produces the 50 in (125 cm) 'Nu Brolly', which represents good value for money.

Many anglers like to retain carp caught during the night for a photograph the following morning. Never put a carp in a keepnet. Indeed, most clubs and fishery owners now insist that carp are either returned to the water immediately or retained in a special carp sack. The majority of commercially made carp sacks are now excellent, although there were a few problems when they first came onto the market. They should be large – at least 3 ft (90 cm) long by 18 in (45 cm) wide – made of soft, dark material and should not restrict water transfer.

Other unusual items I carry in my tackle box, which are essential in an emergency include: scissors, a sharp knife, a small screwdriver, pointed pliers, a small torch, plasters and bandage, Paracetemol tablets, insect repellant and Anthisan ointment. It is also a good idea to include a change of clothes, or at least socks and trousers. It has been known for the occasional angler to take an unexpected bath!

CHAPTER FIVE

LOCATING CARP

The adage 'First find your fish' has been used so many times that I was loath to repeat it yet again. However, it is so important that it just has to be said. Even successful anglers sometimes forget this cardinal rule and can be seen going through the motions of carp fishing with no idea of whether or not there are carp in the vicinity. So many carp anglers fall into a rut with their carp fishing. They arrive at the water after finishing work on a Friday evening, a couple of hours before dark. This allows them almost no time to figure out where carp might be. Guesswork, or where fish were caught the previous weekend, or a comfortable spot to pitch a 'bivvy', are all used to choose swims. This haphazard choice of swim becomes permanent for the weekend for the simple reason that the majority of anglers take far too much unnecessary equipment, making the job of moving an unwelcome chore.

Waters without clues

Of course, there are situations when it is difficult, or even impossible, to determine if fish are resident in, or sometimes pass through, a particular swim. Certain fisheries just do not lend themselves to visual location. One particular clay pit I am familiar with has deep water in the margins, no trees on the banks for a high viewpoint, almost no surface weed in which the carp can bask in hot weather and, to make things even more difficult, the carp do not roll, leap or show themselves very much. This sort of situation can initially be a bit of a lottery and there really is no short-cut to learning about such a water. The bottom features, such as bars and depressions, sunken trees and other obstructions, the weedbeds, the effects of wind, and where other anglers are catching fish, become so much more important when visual location is difficult.

Len Arbery concentrating on small bites, an intense technique best employed during the often productive early-morning period.

Geoff Crawford of York, with a 22 lb (9.9 kg) carp caught from Motorway Pond, fishing boilies over a bed of particle baits.

A specimen mirror carp. Success in carp fishing comes from exploiting the full range of methods.

Tony Arbery and Peter Collins awake to find a hard frost has lessened the likelihood of carp feeding.

Lake Cassien expert, Phil Smith, with the sort of fish for which this huge lake has become renowned. This beauty weighed 48 lb (21.8 kg).

Often, a particular area which provides 'takes' from carp, appears to be no different from the surrounding lake bottom. The 'hot spot' is sometimes no bigger than a dining-room table, yet cast outside this area and you will find bites are few and far between. An example of this happened to some friends of mine who were fishing for carp at Wintersett Reservoir, near Wakefield in Yorkshire. One rod, out of nine fished in close proximity, produced almost all the fish. This situation continued throughout several seasons. There are many possible explanations, such as localized areas of natural food, the presence of bloodworm or mussel beds, or, when the fishery has been constructed by damming a stream, the path of the original stream often attracts the fish.

Sometimes, in very old lakes, particularly small waters surrounded by very many large, deciduous trees, the bed of the lake can become covered in deep, anaerobic sediment. No fish likes to root about in this type of material, and you can understand why when you prod it with a stick. The stinking gases produced by decomposition, smelling of rotten eggs and containing methane and hydrogen sulphide, bubble to the surface.

In such situations an area of contrasting bottom sediment, such as a bank of clean gravel or a clay mound, will be a regular feeding spot for carp. They will, however, adapt to feeding in anaerobic sediment if they have no other choice. Instead of their customary browsing and rooting slowly through the well decayed silt, they tend to suck up a mouthful and quickly swim off, avoiding the release of noxious gases.

Tactics for big-fish waters

Location is always going to be more important, and difficult, on waters which hold big fish. There are several reasons for this. Big-fish waters tend to be somewhat understocked, thereby ensuring maximum growth. On smaller, overstocked fisheries the carp have to search far more widely for food, feeding in all available areas, unless forced out by the pressure of over-fishing. Location is almost always easier on smaller waters, even assuming equal stock density and available natural food. Once a fishery reaches 20–30 acres (8–12 hectares), and unless its shape is long and thin, there will be considerable areas that lie outside of casting range. It is generally accepted that the pressure of intensive carp angling will push carp into those areas which are at the extremities of, or beyond, casting range.

Because the majority of carp on large, pressured fisheries tend to be caught at long range, it is assumed that this is where they spend all their time. This can be part of the story, but what we also face here is fish preferring to take bait in those areas of the lake in which they feel safe. There are a number of things which can make a carp suspicious and refuse to take a bait confidently. These include the smell, taste, texture, size and colour, and also the behaviour of the bait, which, when attached to a hook and line, may respond unusually under examination by a carp. Other less obvious factors which carp may associate with being caught on previous occasions are the time of day, line being visible near the bait and bankside noise.

Wind direction can be a vital key to locating fish. While the effects of wind are often more pronounced on large waters, wind does not always influence the distribution of fish. There existed, before it was shamefully turned into a refuse tip, a small, but interesting, gravel pit near Brandesburton in Yorkshire, called Catwick Pond. In its crystal-clear water lived about thirty large carp. The pond was roughly a flattened oval, lying directly east-west. It was *always* the case that if the wind was blowing towards the eastern end then *all* the carp would be there, and if the wind was in the other direction then *all* the carp would be at the western end. I have never come across another fishery where the carp were so invariably influenced by the wind. Conversely, on a large, open clay pit near Newport in North Humberside, wind appears to have little or no influence on the movement of the carp.

Clearly, wind can play an important role in fish movement, at least on some waters, and this possibility must be one of the first factors to consider, particularly if visual observation of the carp is limited. Why and how the wind affects these movements is open to debate. Coloured water caused by strong wave action may be a reason. Certainly fish do sometimes feel more secure, and feed well, in coloured water. A strong wind can increase the amount of dissolved oxygen in the water and, particularly in very hot weather, or if the wind precedes overcast, humid conditions, this can encourage feeding. Strong wind also discourages anglers, reducing catches.

They say that carp follow the wind. This 24 lb 10 oz (11 kg) fish did – and was caught by Tricia King 10 yards (9 m) from the bank.

The effects of wind on a medium-sized lake can vary greatly, and depend to a considerable extent on how the wind interacts with surrounding valleys and hills, bankside tree cover, islands, underwater bars and even weedbeds. On large waters, particularly those with a uniform depth, an undertow can develop. The water at the surface is pushed along in the same direction as the wind, but on striking the bank it is forced to the bottom and pushed along in the opposite direction to that of the wind.

Long-term effects of wind

In Britain the predominant wind direction is south-westerly. This has important implications, for just as a solitary tree will often grow at an angle, slowly and relentlessly pushed over by the action of regular wind, so that same wind action can gradually mould the features of a lake. On very large lakes, weed growth will be most prolific in those areas least affected by the action of the strong winds which cause unstable bottom sediment in shallow water. On smaller lakes and ponds the opposite tends to occur: the overall, much gentler action of the south-westerly wind pushes floating debris, leaves, twigs and aquatic plant life into the north-east corner and slowly causes a build-up of nutrient-rich detritus. In the absence of the unstable bottom typical of very large waters, weed growth and natural food items often become well established. On extensive lakes, reservoirs and meres which are river fed, the persistent action over a long period of time of the south-westerly wind will cause a build-up of sediment carried by the river or stream at the point where it enters the water. This build-up gradually moves the mouth of the river to one side, often leaving a shallow bay rich in nutrients. These bays, with their rich flora and fauna, are important spawning and feeding areas, as shown in the diagram below.

One of the most importance influences of the predominant south-

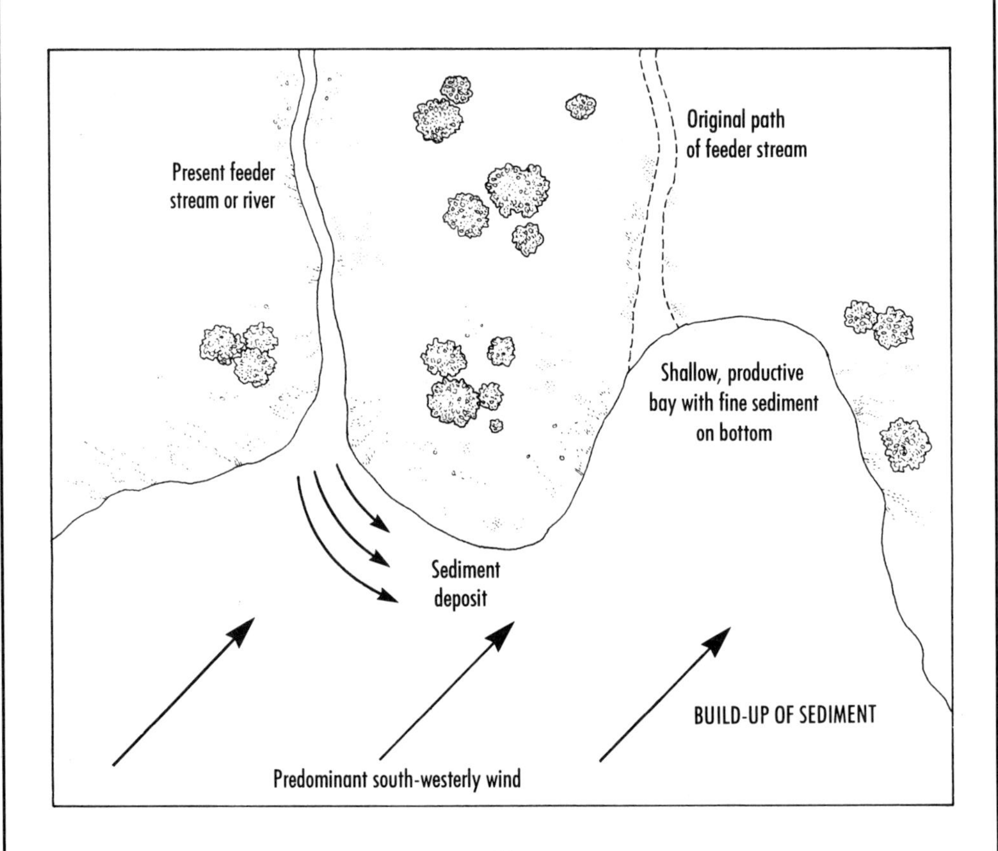

westerly wind is its action on newly dug sand, gravel and clay pits. With the cessation of working, a number of mounds of unusable material usually remain at the bottom of the void. If the mounds are large enough, they become islands when the pit is flooded. Until vegetation becomes firmly established on these islands – and this can take several years – they remain very susceptible to erosion from wave action. This usually causes the islands to develop in a certain way, as the diagram below shows.

Studying the weather

A basic understanding of the factors which affect weather can be very useful. It is a good idea to get into the habit of watching the weather reports on the television each night, when much useful information can be gained. Apart from wind, other weather conditions which can have a marked effect on fishing are cloud, tempera-

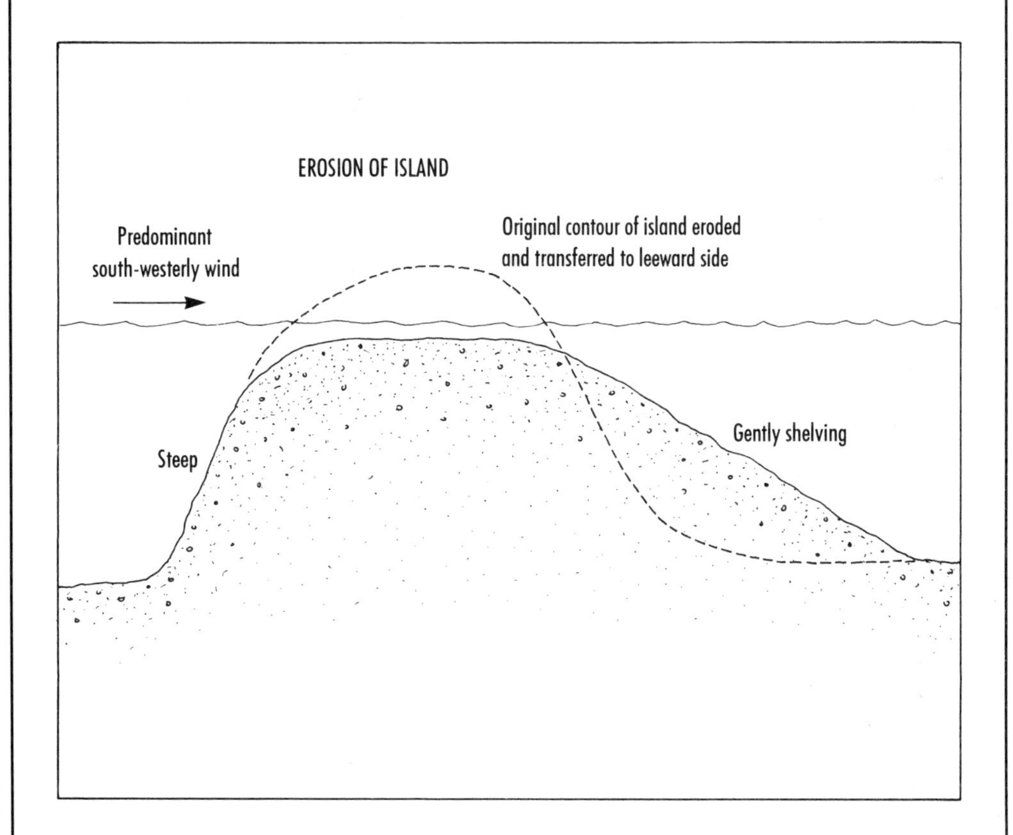

ture and rain. Barometric pressure may also have a direct effect, although there is disagreement about this. It has been suggested that since liquids, including water, are virtually incompressible, barometric pressure cannot be transmitted to fish. However, certain experiments suggest that fish can detect changes in such pressure and it is thought that these are perceived through either the gas-bladder, the Weberian ossicles or the inner ear.

Certain fisheries seem to respond to particular weather conditions or sequences of weather. Generalizations are risky, but some obvious examples follow. In lakes which are small, shallow, mud-bottomed, silty, tree-lined, and where oxygen levels probably fall during prolonged hot (perhaps anti-cyclonic) periods, a sudden change to cooler, cloudy weather with strong winds and perhaps rain will almost certainly stimulate the carp to begin feeding avidly. Conversely, on a large, deepish, clear gravel pit, with lots of aquatic vegetation, a prolonged period of hot weather often results in the carp feeding very well, often in the shallower water. So understanding how weather can affect specific fisheries is tremendously important. Prior knowledge of sudden weather changes may allow you to take advantage of such opportunities. A couple of days off work mid-week to coincide with the weather change, when few other anglers are present, may well give you the chance to make the most of a frenzied feeding spell which might occur only a few times each season.

The Meteorological Office in Britain provides a comprehensive, local three-to-six-day forecast through its Weathercall service. This is obtained by dialling 0898 500 followed by the regional code in the right-hand column below:

Greater London	401
Kent, Surrey, Sussex	402
Dorset, Hants, IoW	403
Devon, Cornwall	404
Wiltshire, Glos, Avon, Somserset	405
Berks, Buck, Oxon	406
Beds, Herts, Essex	407
Norfolk, Suffolk, Cambs	408
Glamorgan, Gwent	409
Shropshire, Hereford & Worcs	410

Signs of feeding

During the first few visits to a water, especially if you know little about the feeding areas, it is worth choosing a swim which gives an excellent view over as much of the fishery as possible. You are then able to fish and look for evidence of feeding carp. Signs to watch for are fish regularly leaping in the same area; 'rolling', when you just see the top of the head, the back and a bit of the fish's tail; 'bubbling', which is caused by carp digging in the bottom sediment and releasing gases of decomposition; and coloured water resulting from the disturbance of the lake bed by feeding fish.

Of course, you need to be sure that all these signs are caused by carp, and not by some other species of fish. Large 'rolling' bream have often been mistaken for carp, and other species can be responsible for 'bubbling' and coloured water. Some lake bottoms periodically give off confusing bursts of bubbles. This is often the case where there is a lot of decomposing sediment, particularly smaller lakes and ponds such as estate lakes and waters surrounded by many trees. Only experience can teach an angler to tell the difference between natural releases of gas and those caused by fish. But obviously, in a gravel pit or clay pit, where natural escapes of gas do not occur regularly, continuous releases of patches of bubbles, either in a small area or in a specific path, can be assumed to be caused by fish. The species responsible are usually carp or tench, and sometimes bream.

Any high vantage point will greatly assist in the visual location of carp. High banks, fences, trees, telegraph poles and even the top of a car have all proved useful. Binoculars and Polaroid sunglasses are essential – without them many fish will be missed. Often fish can be seen from the bank, but it is extremely important to approach them with care. They have excellent eyesight and are extremely sensitive to vibrations. Use any natural cover available and make as little of yourself visible as possible. Take it slowly, with no sudden movements.

If at first you see nothing, wait, and keep looking. Carp often merge very well with their surroundings. They are frequently hidden among dense aquatic vegetation, and if you look very carefully you may suddenly spot part of a tail, or just a pair of lips sticking out. Carp found 'lying up' in dense weedbeds, although not actively feeding, will often be prepared to take a bait. Any situation which gives the carp a feeling of security, whether it be dense weed, snags or being tucked under the overhanging branches of a tree, tends to make it react to a bait less suspiciously.

Underwater topography

Apart from the above methods of location, there is another which, although regularly recommended by angling writers, is rarely put into practice. Those anglers who do undertake the exercise of mapping out the underwater contours of the water generally have the most success (see diagram opposite). One definition of genius is the ability to take infinite pains, which is another way of saying you get out of fishing what you put in!

The easiest method of gaining a picture of the underwater topography is by using an echo sounder in a boat. Echo sounders vary in price from about £80 for a model which gives a straightforward digital depth read-out, to those costing over £2,000 which have colour screens showing the contours of the bottom. These can also distinguish fish species by portraying them in differing colours, but are really intended for use at sea. An ideal choice for freshwater would

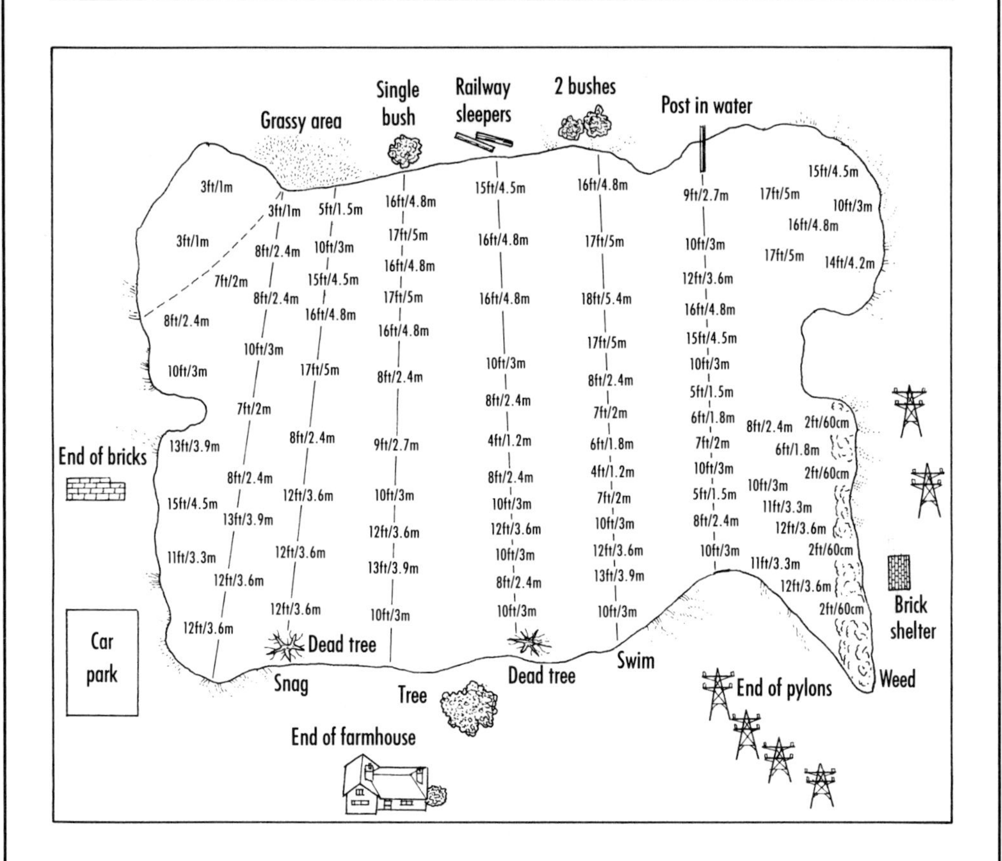

be the well-tested Lowrance 'Eagle Mach 1'. This gives a chart read-out and can differentiate between bottom materials, such as weed, gravel and mud. Individual fish are also displayed, even when they are only about 6 in (15 cm) in length. The drawback is the price, which is about £500. However, with intelligent use, and a little logical guesswork, it is possible to glean almost as much information from models costing far less. A couple of hours with an echo sounder will provide more knowledge of where the fish feed than the majority of anglers assimilate over years of fishing.

Some fishery owners and associations do not allow boats on their waters, but a courteous approach to the owner or secretary, asking for permission to carry out a survey of this kind in the close season, and offering to supply a copy of the results, will sometimes receive a sympathetic response.

The alternative is to use a rod and line. This technique is much slower, not as precise, and you cannot learn as much about the bottom's composition, but it is still very useful. There are some very inexpensive products produced, which claim to give accurate depth readings. These are small tube affairs which work on the principle of water pressure and are often combined with a thermometer. I have one in my tackle box but have rarely used it. Like most of the small number of anglers who take the trouble of finding out the contours of the waters they fish, I almost always use one or other of the two following methods.

The first method, shown in the diagram below, involves a polystyrene, or balsa, float about the size and shape of a large pike bung. It is cut in half, from top to bottom, and a small recess is formed for a piece of bent ballpoint-pen tube. The float is then glued back

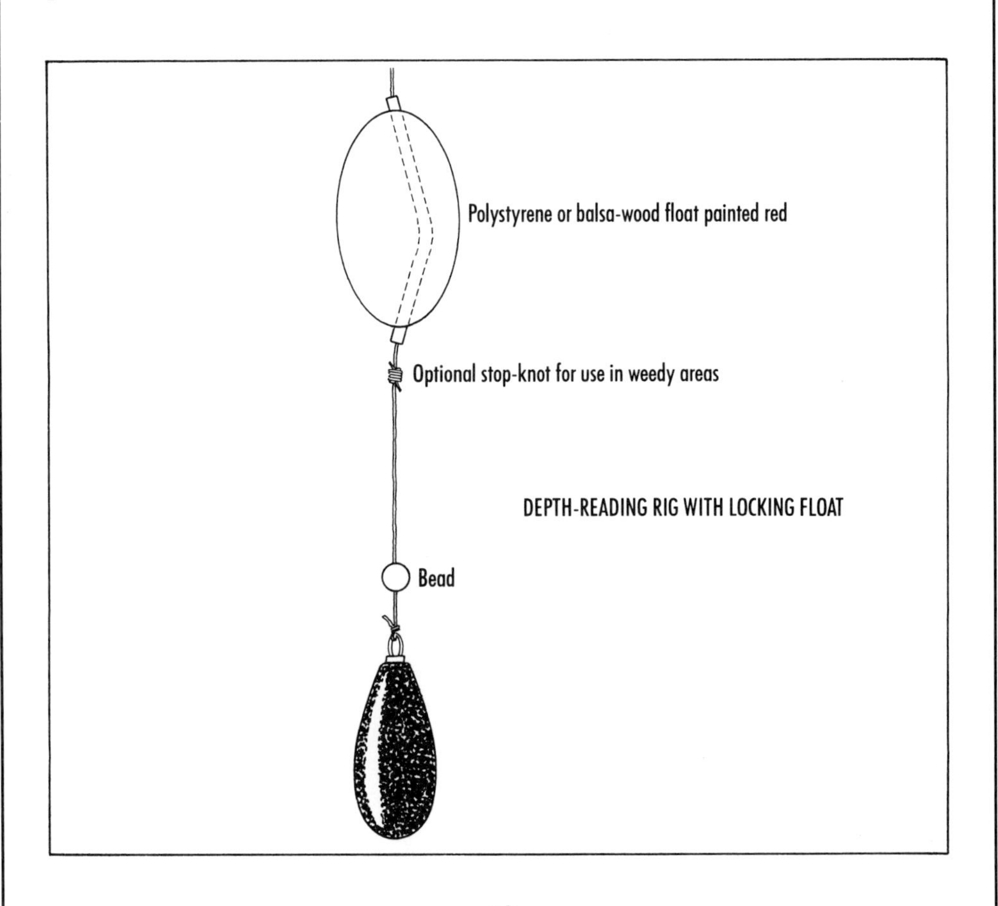

DEPTH-READING RIG WITH LOCKING FLOAT

together, using a waterproof glue such as Araldite, with the tube inside. In use, the line passes through the float and is attached to a large lead weight of at least 2 oz (60 g). When cast out, on a slack line, the float rises to the surface, whereupon the line is tightened and reeled in. This causes the line to be locked in position by the sharp angle of the tube within the float. Providing the line is kept taut on the retrieve, the depth can be gauged accurately. If the line is marked with nail varnish or type-correcting fluid at intervals of a yard (1 m), the marks can be counted on the retrieve to give a good estimate of distance from the bank.

The other method requires a similarly sized float and a large lead. After casting, the free-running float is tightened down until the lead is felt, as in the diagram below. Line is then pulled from the reel in measured amounts. If the distance between the reel spool and the

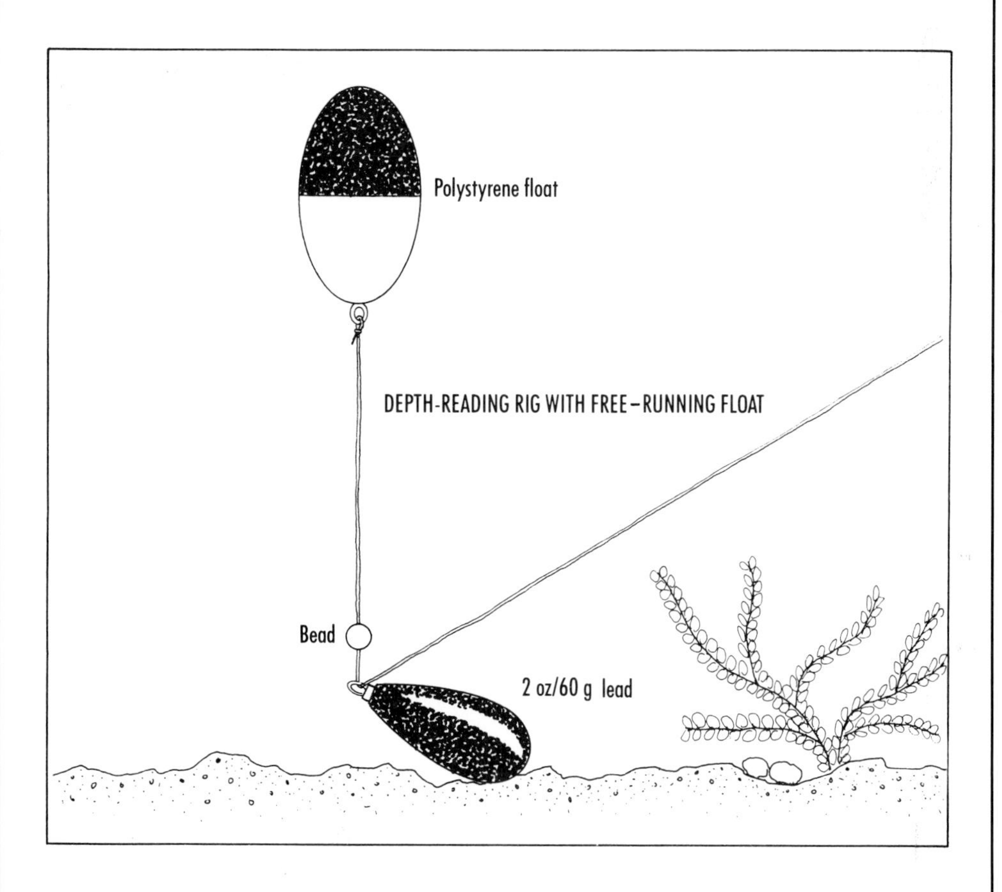

The classic lines of a common carp taken at Redmire by the author. Beauty of this sort makes up for all the blank days.

first rod ring is known exactly, it is a simple matter to count the number of times line is pulled between these two points before the float appears on the surface. One drawback is that this method does not work well in weedy conditions since the eye of the lead tends to get clogged up. The first technique is superior in this respect because the float will stay up the line, above the weed depth, before you cast.

It is a good idea to transfer all the information onto a plan as soon as possible, otherwise it will be forgotten or distorted with the passage of time.

CHAPTER SIX

BAITS

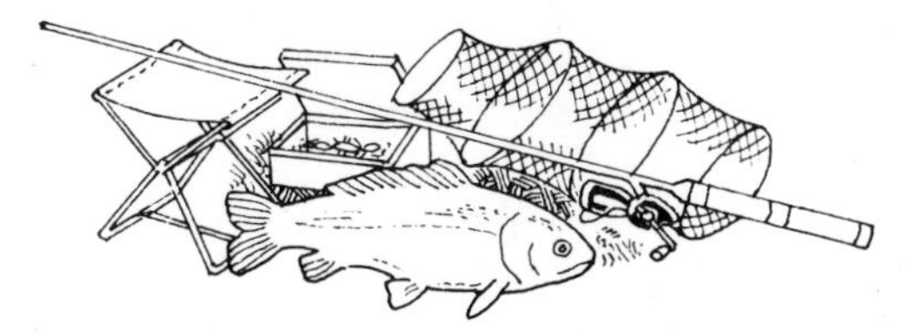

When I began carp fishing some twenty years ago, the secrecy, the mystique, the awe of the sport were mostly focused on waters. Whispered tales of 30 lb (14 kg) carp being caught from a gravel pit near Staines, or rumours on the grapevine about big fish coming from an estate lake in Lincolnshire, was the sort of talk that could be expected when carp anglers got together. False names given to waters to obscure their identity and smoke-screens to send the unwary off on a wild-goose chase were all part of the game. How many times has a carp angler started a sentence with, 'If you promise not to tell anyone else . . .'? For that matter, how many times have I said it myself? The silliness of it all, for how can we expect another to keep a secret if we have been unable to keep it ourselves?

Nowadays with the very welcome wider distribution of big carp, plus the fact that the majority of carp waters are generally known about, the mystique of the sport has transferred to the subject of baits. This change in emphasis is shown clearly in a comparison between two books about carp fishing, both written by very fine anglers. *Carp*, written by Jim Gibbinson in 1968, contained some 2 per cent specifically about baits. Kevin Maddocks in his *Carp Fever*, published in 1981, devoted almost a quarter of it to baits.

I suppose it is part of human nature to perpetuate the belief that some small item of information, known only to the chosen few, can vastly improve your ability in a given field. Those occasions when this happens to be the case only serve to strengthen this generally held conviction. Claims of near-magical properties for fishing baits are nothing new. From the time of Izaak Walton various ingredients and essences have been suggested as the key to success, among them aniseed, tar, honey, liquidized worms, bullocks' brains and bait soaked in brandy and purgatives! No doubt some caught carp while

Swan mussels are out of fashion, yet are both effective and cheap.

others did not. Much the same applies today, but with an added complication. During the last ten years, commercial interests have responded to the dramatic increase in carp angling by offering a wide variety of carp baits and bait ingredients. The quality and effectiveness of these range from first-class to rubbish.

Before the carp-fishing revolution of the early 1960s the angling pressure on carp waters was negligible and there was little or no motivation to develop carp baits beyond those which had proved successful up until that time. But with the popularization of the sport, inspired by the exploits of Dick Walker and his friends, the increased demands put on certain waters, notably those in Kent, resulted in carp becoming highly 'educated' and suspicious of baits in general use, particularly bread, worms and potatoes. The new breed of young, success-hungry carp anglers soon started experimenting with various alternatives, leaving us twenty-five years later with a variety of baits which can leave newcomers perplexed.

It is difficult to allocate baits exactly to specific groups, but there is a general acceptance of the following categories.

Natural baits

The most commonly used baits in this category are maggots and worms, both of which have taken some very big fish and catches of carp. They are not used so much nowadays but their effectiveness in stalking and casting to feeding carp in the margins is well proven. I learnt this lesson the hard way, in the early 1970s at Waterways, near Hemingford Grey, by watching experts in this style of fishing, such as Duncan Kay and John Dennis, continually outcatch my ledgered 'boilies'. Some waters respond to this type of fishing, particularly smaller, shallower, clear waters with overgrown, tree-lined banks.

Other natural baits which have caught carp include wasp grubs, meal-worms, snails, slugs, casters, shrimps, caterpillars, mussels, cockles, leeches, crayfish, beetles, silkworms, tadpoles, dragonfly larvae, caddis-fly larvae, tubifex worms and fish eggs.

Conventional baits

These include readily available items such as bread, cheese, luncheon meat, potato, banana, marshmallow, Plumrose 'Bacon Grill', and salami.

Paste baits

The development of paste baits began in the early 1960s. At first, luncheon-meat paste and sausage-meat paste, which had long been successful baits for chub and barbel, were used. By the latter part of the decade numerous variations had been tried, many of which initially caught a lot of fish. Some of the most popular, used through the late 1960s and early 1970s, were: cat- and dog-food pastes (my

A fine bag of carp all over 10 lb (4.5 kg) and all caught on sausage-meat paste at Brandesburton Ponds, in Yorkshire, in 1971.

personal favourites were Pedigree Chum and Kit-e-Kat), tinned sardine and pilchard paste, trout-pellet paste, fish-roe paste (either purchased from a wet fish shop or canned), Campbell's meat balls (the meat balls were used on the hook and the gravy used to make paste baits for groundbaiting), proprietary pastry mix and meat-pâté pastes. A multitude of flavours were added to these baits – gravy browning, peanut butter, Oxo cubes, curry powder, meat extracts, maple syrup, cod-liver oil and Marmite – with the intention of making them more attractive to carp. However, the loose consistency of many of these ingredients required the addition of some form of binding agent. At first, bread groundbait, flour, rusk, semolina and ground rice were used.

Although the development of these paste baits resulted in improved catches, they did have a few drawbacks. They were equally attractive to other fish, such as bream and tench, and even large baits could eventually be whittled down and taken by smaller species, particularly roach and eels. It was also inevitable that the carp would become 'educated' and suspicious of many such baits.

High-nutritional-value (HNV) baits and 'boilies'

A fresh approach, with some original thinking, was supplied by Fred Wilton of Kent. Although Fred was an angler, his main hobby was chemistry. He had read of an Australian scientist who had discovered that most of the rabbits in that country were deficient in certain blood salts and that they would chew wooden stakes impregnated with the equivalent substances. Fred wondered if the same might apply to carp. Over a number of years he developed this line of thought and came up with the principle on which the majority of carp baits are now based.

The idea is to create a bait with a high nutritional value. These so-called HNV baits (also referred to as high-protein baits) are generally based on milk protein, either casein or calcium caseinate (Casilan) and lactalbumin. However, other proteins, for example those derived from vegetables, such as soya isolate or gluten, and artificially manufactured protein, such as Pruteen, have also been used. Minerals and vitamins are added, using products such as Equivite and Phillips' Yeast Mixture.

Nowadays, some sort of smell and/or flavouring is also usually

Fred Wilton's revolutionary P.Y.M. bait accounted for this very pretty 14 lb (6.5 kg) carp from a Midlands gravel pit.

added. This effect is achieved by using all manner of ingredients, ranging from neat chemicals to naturally occurring oils. In general, the majority of flavours are commercial preparations manufactured for the human food industry. These are readily obtainable, as are all of the products necessary to make HNV baits, from many tackle shops and retail bait suppliers. Other useful sources of bait ingredients are health-food shops, foreign food shops and delicatessens, chemists, some pet stores, and animal-feed suppliers.

Fred Wilton's other stroke of genius was to add eggs to the final dry mix. This enables the bait to be rolled into balls and boiled, giving a bait a durable skin which makes it virtually immune to the attentions of most other fish. The success and popularity of this concept has resulted in 'boilies' being used for the vast majority of carp fishing today. Indeed, it has created the establishment of a number of independent, bait-ingredient suppliers and several producers of ready-made 'boilies'.

One of the most intriguing questions concerning baits is whether HNVs actually work for the reasons claimed. Can fish really appreciate that what they are eating is good for them? Can they, in some instinctive way, choose a balanced diet if given the choice? Objective evidence is rather sparse, and understandably so, for outside the laboratory the variables involved cloud the overall picture. At best, only impressions can be gained. The carp world is clearly divided on this. Eminent authorities protest that the idea is bunkum. Some simply profess scepticism, while those who sit on the fence avoid the possible embarrassment of being wrong. Plenty have changed their opinions and others have continued to preach the dogma. Tim Paisley has a particular interest in HNV baits and gives his views on their merits and drawbacks below.

WHY DO HNV BAITS WORK? BY TIM PAISLEY

Let us start by looking at this word 'nutritional'. It derives of course from 'nutrition', which is defined in the dictionary as 'involving the intake and assimilation of nutrient materials'. We eat to survive and if what we eat is not nutritional our health suffers. What do we need to eat? We require nutrients, comprising protein, carbohydrate, fats, vitamins, minerals and fibre. How do we know what to eat?

Because we were taught at school and by our parents or guardians.

We take what we eat for granted but if we sit down and think about what we consume, we find that, generally, we eat a balanced diet. Meat, potatoes and two veg! It may be boring, but such food is good for you and contains all the important nutrients. With an unbalanced diet, which we tend to adopt when we are given freedom of choice and are able to indulge our bad eating and drinking habits, we start to lose our shape and our fitness. What has all this got to do with carp and carp baits? Well, ignore this word 'bait' for the moment because it causes confusion. Concentrate on the concept of fish and their food sources. The attitude of anglers towards baits, apart from carp specialists, is quite simple. In all probability the only baits that are considered are maggots, worms, bread, luncheon meat, sweetcorn and various groundbaits. They are all foods, and all are definable in terms of nutrients. These nutrients are mainly protein, carbohydrate, fat/protein, lipids/carbohydrate, and carbohydrate plus. You can say that it is all nonsense and they are just bait! But then how come all the baits are foods?

A selective diet

That bait is food is undeniable. The major difficulty comes when you first encounter the suggestion that something supposedly as unintelligent as a fish can select its food on the basis of its nutritional value. In other words, a nutritional bait will prove more successful than a non-nutritional one. No angler who has been fishing for carp for any length of time will try to argue that carp will eat anything, because we know they will not. The carp's senses tell it what is food and what is not. Some food it will try, but not accept as a regular source; other food it will accept grudgingly; while still other types of food it will accept totally and feed on avidly. If carp cannot think, they cannot make a voluntary choice. They can only select involuntarily as their senses guide them. Analyse any food that carp accept over a period of time and you will find that it contains at least some nutrients needed by the fish.

Having established the basic fact that carp only eat food, let us change direction for a moment and examine what is, to some, a twilight area – the idea that animals have an instinctive recognition of those food sources that best fulfil their nutritional requirements.

This instinctive capability can be unique to types of animals, and to species within that type, to a very noticeable degree.

For an example of involuntary instincts at work within individual animal types, consider the following. Cows eat grass. Not some cows, or most cows, but all cows. Their systems are designed to cope with it efficiently; their instincts make them eat it. Virtually no birds eat grass, no matter how hungry they are (the few exceptions are geese and some ducks). Why do birds migrate? Because it gets cold? Apparently not. Those birds that migrate do so because they can only find food when it is light and they cannot survive more than twelve hours without feeding. So most of them vanish in September, at about the time of the autumnal equinox. Instinct again. Have you got a garden? If you have never seen greenfinches in it put out some seeds, in particular peanuts (human grade) and greenfinches will usually appear within a couple of days. Grow those tall thistles with seed pods like the Scottish national emblem and you will attract goldfinches in the autumn. Put slightly rotting apples out in the late autumn and winter and they will be eaten – but only by blackbirds!

There are no thought processes involved in any of the examples cited here – just animals being guided by their instincts. The examples are simple, but I could quote innumerable far more complex cases.

The origins of HNV baits

It is important to understand the circumstances in which the original HNV baits came into existence. The principle was considered by Fred Wilton and the necessary requirements were assessed. (He knew that he had to discover what carp's natural food-source nutrients were before he could come up with a bait that would appeal to their instincts.) A bait fulfilling those requirements was put together, research having shown him that carp need protein, selected vitamins, some minerals and fats in their diet (a number of scientific papers suggest that they have a limited nutritional capability with carbohydrates) – and it worked.

In carp fishing it is always easy to be wise after the event. Once you are given the knowledge, derived from a big breakthrough, then put it into practice and catch carp, it is all too easy to ignore the mistakes, heartaches, frustrations and tremendous effort that went into establishing that principle. Fred Wilton's baits were based on no existing carp fishing doctrine. They were founded on natural laws. And even then, putting the theory into practice was not easy. Fred must have known from his reading that casein was the best protein for carp. The problem was that there was no casein readily available at that time – so Fred manufactured his own! There was no ideal vitamin and mineral mix available, so again he made his own. He knew that the theory was right and went to enormous lengths to come up with the bait that would take advantage of the scientific truth underlying his investigations.

I have laboured this area somewhat – intentionally – because the theory was there already. The principle existed and was understood before the bait was invented. So when you are confronted for the first time with the fact of HNVs, if you react with scorn, insisting that carp cannot know the difference, as thousands (me included) have, you are not casting any doubt on the validity of the scientifically proven relationship between carp and their food sources. You are simply displaying your own profound ignorance of the subject. You cannot refute scientific fact except by disproving it on a scientific and practical basis.

Efficient senses

Nature equips all wild creatures with the senses and instincts to locate and assimilate those nutrients they require for survival. A carp requires protein, fats, vitamins and minerals to sustain it. Therefore nature designed it to recognize these nutrients, be they in the shape of insect life, luncheon meat or whatever other form the food source may take. Think about how a carp eats naturally and you will begin to grasp why its senses have to be so efficient. A carp is not a sight-feeder, as the pike is. It feeds by smell and taste, and ingests its food by the mouthful, that mass usually including a high percentage of mud, weed and water in addition to the animal matter which the fish's system selects and digests. The quality of the nutrients in this animal matter will be high and the conversion rate will be good, because the food source comes complete with its own active enzymes to supplement those of the carp. A nutrient is a nutrient: you must look to the scientific breakdown of a food to assess its nutritional value, not to a vague description.

Objections to HNV baits

In addition to the 'Carp can't tell the difference' chestnut, two other major arguments are used against HNVs. One is that they do not always work. The other is that at times carp will apparently eat anything, often in very large quantities. They are both valid points, but neither is at odds with the principles of HNVs.

In order to understand why these baits work, you must first understand why they do not, or might not, work. Strictly speaking, rather than saying 'not work', it would be more accurate to say that there are times when they are more effective than they are at others. A bait does not have to fulfil our definition of a high-nutritional-value bait to be nutritional to carp. We eat to satisfy a basic hunger; carp eat to satisfy a nutritional need. Through June, July and August they feed on those food sources with which they are most familiar. Their major requirement at this time of the year is to build up energy reserves depleted by the rigours of surviving the winter and the spawning season (which must be a massive drain on energy reserves compared to the demands of a carp's normal sedentary existence). Any energy source is of high nutritional value in such circumstances. During those summer months natural food is at its most abundant, supplying whatever protein is required. High-fat (energy) sources such as seeds and particles are in demand. Fats are the best energy sources; carbohydrates are limited energy sources (to carp); proteins are energy sources, but are wasted if they have to be utilized as such. The principal nutritional requirement of all animals is the fulfilment of the day-to-day need for energy. Any carp bait that satisfies that energy requirement, in full or in part, can be called nutritional.

Seasonal nutritional needs

So why bother with the expensive proteins, finding the right vitamin and mineral combination, adding a nutritional fat source, then going to the trouble of trying to establish an HNV bait, when you can catch carp on much simpler alternatives? Because a carp's nutritional requirements change with the time of year. Protein-based HNV baits will catch throughout the fishing season, but their effectiveness increases from the end of August onwards. If you are using an HNV from the start of the season, make sure it has a high vegetable oil content. Carp will rarely rely on one food source, but the greater the deficiencies of your bait the greater their need will be to feed on sources other than what you are offering.

By September, at the latest, the carp's systems should have caught up with the early-season energy deficiency – and natural protein sources are now diminishing. The early protein intake will have been used for repairing any wastage, or damage, caused by spawning. Protein now starts to come into its own and will be used for growth. Carp are at their heaviest from the end of September onwards, and may continue to put on weight for as long as they continue to eat into the colder months. Through the autumn and winter, HNVs are at their most effective compared with other food sources, because the carp's nutritional need for them is at its greatest. The carp does not understand any of that, any more than the swallow knows why it flies south at the end of September, or blackbirds know why they eat apples. Animals live their lives according to the dictates of their senses and instincts.

As HNV baits are a food source, emphasis must be laid on the quality of the food. The strength of the source of attraction within the bait is important only inasmuch as the attractors must not detract from the bait as a medium-to-long-term food source. If you are fishing HNVs do not think in terms of a result on the first introduction of the bait to the water. You have to give the carp's system time to assess the value of your offerings as a food source. The carp then has to acquire confidence about eating that food source. (I am not absolutely sure of the accuracy of that statement. I sense that the assessment is as instantaneous as it is with, say, cats, but with carp in pressured waters you need the added stimulus of familiarity with the food source in order to overcome their increasing suspicion of anything new that is introduced.) Once you have weaned the carp onto the bait you can apply your energies to catching the fish.

I get a great deal of correspondence about proteins and HNV baits and there are recurring patterns to their successful and unsuccessful use. If you do not feel you are getting the best out of your HNV bait, you may find the reason among the following points.

1 An HNV bait must be considered a food source for it to function at its best. A pound (0.45 kg) of bait per week will only establish

A 20 lb (9 kg) carp caught by the author on a Richworth Tutti-Frutti 'boilie' in conjunction with a PVA stringer on a hair rig.

itself as a bait in circumstances where there is very little competition from other food sources (natural and other baits). The length of time it takes the carp to start accepting your bait confidently will depend on a number of factors, but provided you get the feeding location right they will eat it from the start. Steady application will increase their confidence, but there are no hard-and-fast rules as to how soon full effectiveness is reached. I have known really effective, heavily applied HNVs which went on to take a great many fish without modification, fail to catch for over two weeks. On the other hand, I have caught on them with the first cast. In the first instance the anglers were fishing against well-established, quality baits on a rather difficult water. In the second instance I got lucky. The norm lies somewhere between those two time limits, given the variety in angling pressure, ease of location and availability of natural food supplies.

2 Artificial flavours may limit the life of an HNV bait and a great many successful HNV users rely on alternative attractors or brands. Essential oils and the liquid-protein foods available from health-food shops and bait dealers (Nutramino, Aquamino, Catchum, Sense Appeal, for example) all make good HNV bait additives because they both add to the food value of the bait and attract the fish. Commercial flavours attract, but those based on artificial solvents can reduce the life of the bait by lessening its acceptability as a food. A number of people have suggested to me that it is a good idea to start baiting-up with an increased level of attraction, then gradually reduce it. That is totally self-defeating. The initial stronger smell may have an unacceptable taste, stopping the carp feeding on the bait. That way you ruin the bait's chances before you even get round to fishing it. Bait is food – carp do not eat smells. The fish tell you whether you are getting the bait right or not – not the angling books and the bait recipes. Acceptable attraction levels vary enormously from water to water. If you are sure of the food value of the bait and the carp do not accept it, or stop accepting it, then the attraction level could well be at fault.

3 Do not underestimate the degree to which the carp's nutritional awareness functions. If you are half-hearted about putting together an HNV your lack of application may well let you down. If you are

planning to use HNVs you must believe totally in the principle and go to as much trouble as time and money permit to come up with the best possible bait.

4 Apply as much common sense as possible to the preparation of your bait. I am obsessive about alien smells on my hands when making bait and when handling it at the water. Furthermore, I am convinced that some people fail to catch because of their occupations. I do not decorate within weeks of making baits or going fishing. If I have to check the oil or put petrol in the car I do it at any time other than when I am on the way to a session. Always use fresh ingredients, fresh eggs, and exact measures of everything. Keep to the same mixing, boiling, standing and freezing patterns. Having found the right formula, stick to it rigidly.

5 No bait catches for you – it helps you catch. A bait that the carp want will give you a great deal more help than a bait they are indifferent to, or do not want at all.

Bait size

The food composition of a bait is a nutritional principle; bait size is an angling principle. Comparing a bed of tiny hempseeds, or a bed of tiger nuts, to a bed of medium-coin-sized HNVs is a meaningless exercise. If you want the 'ultimate bait' you must look at its physical and its nutritional properties. Such a bait will be an all-fulfilling, natural-food-imitating HNV in a format similar to rapeseed, but preferably as active as a bed of maggots! It speaks volumes for the effectiveness of modern baits and presentation that wary, educated carp continue to get caught on baits of ¾–1 in (2–2.5 cm) in diameter. In the 1970s we wisely conceded that there were many waters where carp would never be caught on paste baits again.

Protein/fat/vitamin/mineral HNVs are big-fish baits, and you need not use them unless you are after big fish. I shall not define 'big fish', apart from saying that if you fish a water where the carp reach a ceiling of, say, 15 lb (7 kg), a 19–20 lb (8.5–9 kg) fish is big. As such it needs good food. Most big-fish waters are rich in natural food. The bigger fish in such waters may have reached their size because their instincts for good food sources are better developed than those of their smaller brethren.

Big carp need, are capable of recognizing, and eat good food. Come up with the right food of your own and you can catch the bigger fish. Success of this sort will also serve to confirm that you have got all the other aspects of your fishing right. HNVs have been catching for nearly twenty years now, a very long time for anything to work with fickle, quick-to-learn carp. But then how could they 'unlearn' an instinct that has been ruling their systems and feeding habits for thousands of years?

It comes across clearly that Tim has great belief in the HNV bait principle and it is a fact that he has put a tremendous amount of research and thought into this aspect of carp fishing. It has to be said, however, that a body of experienced carp anglers are not completely convinced by the claims made on behalf of such baits. That they can be very successful in catching fish is not in doubt, but the reasons for that success have not been adequately demonstrated. It is probably impossible to do so in the natural environment.

Adaptable diet

The exact scientific evaluation of a carp's nutritional requirements has not been achieved, and indeed it is possible that these requirements may vary between individuals of the same species. Until such an evaluation is carried out, the chances of carp anglers achieving the precise combination in a bait are very slight. The principle put forward by Tim and others tells us that carp will instinctively find their nutritional requirements from natural food sources. I do not necessarily disagree with that statement, but would change the emphasis by saying that it is likely that the species has evolved so that it can satisfy its nutritional requirements from what is available naturally in the environment.

However, there is less ground for agreement when Tim takes his argument a step further by claiming that the bigger fish in rich waters may have grown bigger because their instincts for good food sources are better developed than those of their smaller companions. Fish kept in artificial conditions (in trout farms, intensive carp farming and aquaria) and having an identical food source (the same combination of nutrients) also show variations in growth. Some individual fish eat more than others. If they eat more they grow bigger.

It is really as simple as that. Fish which are selectively bred, such as carp and trout, show a much wider variation in growth than wild fish and it has nothing whatsoever to do with individual fish being able to instinctively identify food items that are nutritionally better than others.

Tim also makes the point that carp have a limited nutritional capability with carbohydrate, and I understand that this view derives from a suggestion that carp are diabetic. Tim's source is a book entitled *Recent Advances in Aquaculture*, which says, 'It suffices to say at this point that no definitive study, has to date, adequately demonstrated the efficacy of dietary carbohydrate as an energy source.' This is a very controversial claim. It is at odds with the generally accepted scientific opinion relating to carbohydrate nutrition in fish; it makes a mockery of generations of carp farming practice, in which high-carbohydrate artificial feed is claimed to have increased yield; and, in my view at least, it does not make common sense. We have a good idea what carp feed on naturally. Examination of the carp's digestive tract tells us that it is an omnivore, although in waters rich in a variety of food sources carp almost certainly derive the bulk of their nutritional needs from animal life.

CHEMICAL COMPOSITION OF NATURALLY OCCURRING FOOD ITEMS IN THE CARP'S DIET

FOOD ITEM	COMPOSITION BY PERCENTAGE			
	Water	Pure protein	Carbohydrate	Fat
Daphnia pul. (water flea)	90.67	1.47	4.07	0.61
Daphnia mag. (water flea)	91.60	2.98	2.63	0.62
Chironomus gr. (midge larva)	87.18	6.21	2.42	1.40
Tubifex (worms)	87.15	4.23	1.88	2.00
Planorbis pl. (snail)	73.00	7.10	8.72	6.95
Anabolia (caddis-fly larva)	77.09	8.61	5.06	0.95

The table tells us that much of the natural diet of carp consists of carbohydrates. We also know that carbohydrate is digested through the intestine of the carp by the action of various enzymes and broken down, mainly into glucose. It seems strange, therefore, that the carp has evolved on a natural diet, a large part of which consists of carbohydrate, which it can readily convert into a source of energy, glucose, but that this cannot be used as such and has to be wastefully excreted. This process is what happens in diabetes.

It seems equally perverse that, on the one hand, the HNV principle proposes that, to create the 'ultimate bait', we must emulate as far as possible the natural food of the carp, yet Tim tells us, on the other hand, to leave out a large proportion of the natural nutrient intake of carp because they do not need it.

The dangers of HNVs

Whatever the truth regarding HNV baits, it cannot be denied that they have accounted for the capture of a tremendous number of carp in recent years. The determination of the carp's nutritional needs and trying to meet those needs with a bait have become almost a separate hobby for many anglers. I am sure that in some cases the carp fishing is now of secondary importance! However, those who travel this route should think about the welfare of the fish. Read the books and scientific papers on fish nutrition and do not readily accept bankside gossip.

Without doubt, on many waters, a large part of the food intake of carp now comprises anglers' baits. Real dangers are posed by the use of some of the substances involved. Excesses of various nutrients can cause damage and, in extreme cases, death. For example, vitamin excesses have been known to cause in carp impaired growth, liver and kidney damage, lethargy, fragile bones, nausea and death. Carbohydrate excesses have been known to lead to liver and pancreatic-tissue damage. Fat excesses have been known to cause liver and heart damage.

Bait ingredient and 'boilie' suppliers

Catchum 88, Main Road, Legbourne, Louth, Lincs (Tel: 0507–607248)
Terry Eustace, 372 Chester Road, Sutton Coldfield, Birmingham, B73 5BT (Tel: 021–373–6627)
NutraBaits, 95 Main Street, North Anston, Sheffield S31 7BE (Tel: 0909–563597)

Prime Attraction Baits, 7 Sycamore Rise, Berkhampstead, Herts HP4 2JZ (Tel: 0442–871601)
Richworth-Streamselect, The Uplands, Langaller Lane, Cobham Road, Fetcham, Surrey, KT22 9SP
Geoff Kemp, Pilgrims Court, Days Lane, Pilgrims Hatch, Brentwood, Essex (Tel: 0277–74291)
Crafty Catcher, 28 The Cotes, Soham, Cambs CB7 5TU (Tel: 0353–723097)
Specialist Bait Supplies, 35 Ferguson Avenue, Gidea Park, Romford, Essex (Tel: 0708–45689)
Kevin Maddocks Boilies, 1 Bylands Close, Poynton, Cheshire SK12 1UQ

Particle and seed baits

Rod Hutchinson is usually credited with the early development of particle baits for carp, although as is often the case, others were thinking along similar lines at about the same time. While the use of small baits to catch large fish is nothing new, hemp seed having been used with tremendous success for barbel in the past, the reasoning behind their use was, more often than not, vague or lacking.

Some of the more successful particle baits are: sweetcorn, peanuts, tiger nuts, maples, red kidney beans, cockles, buck wheat, hemp seed, chick peas, sultanas, aduki beans, dari seeds, trout pellets, blackeye beans, borlotti beans, rice, cashew nuts, peeled prawns, almonds, tares, maize, hazelnuts, tic beans, baked beans. Among the less successful are: green peas, diced carrots, and blackcurrants and similar fruits.

The concept of these baits is that in size they resemble much of the carp's natural food. Because an individual fish has to consume a vast quantity of this type of bait before it is satiated, there is a reasonable possibility of it becoming preoccupied with it. An advantage of such preoccupation is that it results in a gradual decrease in the fish's caution, for as the number of free offerings a fish eats increases so does its feeling of security. It is possible to overcome the wariness that carp naturally possess and which is reinforced by repeatedly being caught, by the introduction of many thousands of tiny baits.

Another benefit of preoccupying carp is that it tends to hold feeding fish in the baited area for long periods and that, particularly with the very small particles, they consume the bait by sucking up quantities of the bottom sediment (unlike with a large bait, which is sucked in individually), sifting out the food items and expelling the debris. Both these factors – fish remaining in the baited area and colouring up the water – tend to attract additional fish to the area, which are also encouraged to begin feeding. I suspect that when a group of carp are feeding in this manner, there develops a feeling of 'safety in numbers' and this is when opportunities arise to capture several carp in a short period. This type of fishing requires the introduction of large quantities of bait. A 56 lb (25 kg) bag of particles could easily be used up over several days' fishing. I remember introducing half a bag of red dari seeds (about 28 lb/13 kg) close in to Greenbanks, at Redmire Pool, in late summer 1975. Half a dozen big carp ravenously devoured the lot in about two hours!

The value of prebaiting

Most particle and seed baits do not bring 'instant' results in the way that sweetcorn can, but when used in the right circumstances they can be startlingly successful. When introducing a new particle for the first time to a water it is a good idea to carry out prebaiting. As a general rule, the particles with a distinctive flavour, particularly those eaten by humans, produce more immediate results. It is also probably true that the smaller particles have a longer life expectancy.

Suppliers of seeds & beans

Your local commercial telephone directory should list suppliers of seeds and beans under the heading 'Corn and Seed Merchants' or 'Seed Merchants'. If they supply direct to the public, they generally do so in large quantities (minimum usually a 56 lb/25 kg bag) but this does work out as the cheapest way to buy. If they do not, they will give you a list of retail outlets that they supply, mainly pet and animal-feed shops. There are also some bait suppliers who sell seeds and beans. A recommended dealer is: Tony Osborne Particle Baits, 1 Morley Road, Sutton, Surrey (Tel: 01–644–7747).

Dawn on a stillwater fishery. This is one of the most successful times to fish for carp.

Top A fine wild carp.

Above Tricia King returns a 15 lb (6.8 kg) leather carp to Nostell Priory Lake, near Wakefield, a specialist carp fishery.

Even living as far away as Yorkshire, Richard Skidmore had considerable success at the notoriously difficult Wraysbury Pit, in Middlesex, as this fine 20 lb (9 kg) plus mirror carp proves.

An unusual picture of two carp competing at the surface for an angler's floaters.

CHAPTER SEVEN

TACTICS AND TECHNIQUES

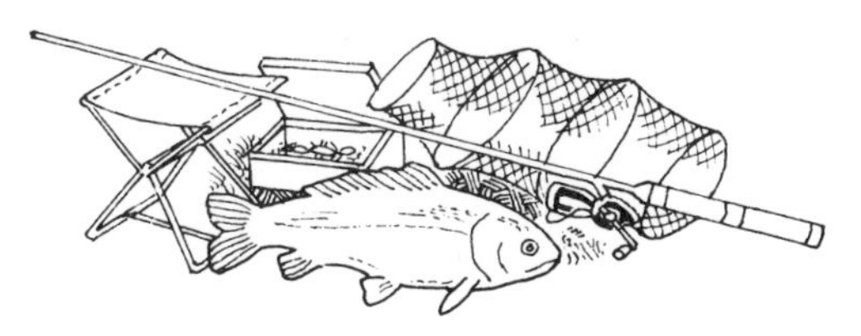

First of all, decide exactly what you want from your carp fishing. If you are not clear, you may face repeated disappointment, which can result in disillusionment with the sport. A lot of young anglers start carp fishing wanting to catch only very large fish. Catching big carp is hard. Few anglers have the time, money, access to waters holding reasonable quantities of big carp, or the determination. Of those that do, only a very small minority stick at it for more than a few years. I can say this without fear of anyone accusing me of 'sour grapes', having caught my fair share of very big carp, after serving my 'apprenticeship'.

It was five years before I caught my first 20 lb (9 kg) carp, but those five years spent catching 'wildies' of 4–5 lb (1.8–2.25 kg) and 'king' carp which barely weighed over 10 lb (4.50 kg) were probably the most enjoyable period in some twenty years of carp fishing. Do not be fooled by the 'macho' image that has been built up in recent years around big-carp fishing.

Fishing is about catching fish. If that means setting your sights a little lower and having some fun at the same time, is that not what a hobby is all about? The majority of carp anglers will, sooner or later, want to try and catch bigger and bigger fish. That is all part of carp fishing, but when the signs of obsession start to show – the disruption of family life, arguments with fishing pals, petty jealousy, 'pulling stunts' and breaking rules to try and give yourself that extra 'edge' – that is the time to sit back and consider your priorities. This advice is not aimed at putting anyone off carp fishing; just the opposite in fact. The purpose is to get people to try and enjoy what is, without doubt, one of the most absorbing, creative and fulfilling of sports.

It is difficult to think of a better way to learn about carp than by actually catching them. Happily, there are lots of waters around

A simple ledger set-up with a swingtip has long been productive with carp. The choice of bait needs careful consideration, though.

nowadays, often fishable on day tickets, which are overstocked with carp. These fish never grow to any tremendous size, but they are generally 'educated', hungry carp that are not too difficult to catch. These types of fisheries are popular both with carp specialists and the ordinary pleasure angler. They offer ideal learning opportunities for budding as well as experienced carp anglers, and for the carp themselves! The beginner will do no better than to start his carp fishing on such a water.

Picking up tips

The more experienced anglers are less secretive when fishing this type of water, and tips about baits and rigs will soon be given to those who ask for advice in a reasonable manner. It will not be long before the beginner is accepted by the 'regulars'. With a bit of luck the tyro will soon be trusted with more privileged and detailed information about the latest bait or how to obtain membership to an exclusive carp pool.

But if you want to be really successful you have to work hard at it. The first job is to use an Ordnance Survey map of the locality to identify all the waters that may hold carp. It is a good idea to keep a notebook along the following lines:

Redstone Lake
Grid reference: SO 543219
Location: 1 mile (1.6 km) east of Glewstone, Hereford and Worcester, near the A4137.
Stocks: Very large carp to 30 lb (14 kg). Stocked around 1930, no recent stocking. About twenty-five fish over 20 lb (9 kg) with a fair head of smaller fish. Also contains some superb big 'common' carp.
Topography: Estate lake, about 3 acres (1.2 hectares). Surrounded by trees. Deepest point off dam approx. 11 ft (3.5 m). Lots of weed. Three islands.
Control: Syndicate run by Mr Jack Hinlot, 117 Low Road, Wortwell, Norfolk.
Comments: Lake regularly fished by experienced carp anglers. Fish difficult but size (particularly of 'commons') makes it desirable. Applied to join 13 September 1982.

Willow Water
Grid reference: SE 721502
Location: North-east of Pocklington, near Burnby, North Humberside.
Stocks: No large carp yet present. Recent stocking (1986) of 400 small 'mirror' carp (about 2 lb/0.9 kg). Fish growing fast; caught up to 8 lb (3.5 kg) in autumn 1988.
Topography: Gravel pit of about 20 acres (8 hectares). Various depths to maximum 25 ft (8 m). Very open, little bankside cover. Some bottom weed along north bank. Gravel extraction ceased in 1972.
Control: Pocklington & District AC – Open membership £10 per year. Apply: The Secretary, Mr Rudd, 44 Redmire Close, Hitchin, Herts (enclose s.a.e.).
Comments: Tremendous potential in a few years' time. Keep close watch on developments. May be worth joining next season, because once large carp start being caught, in three or four years' time, there will be a rush of applications from carp anglers from far and wide. Since this is the only water run by this small local angling club, it is very likely they will at some stage restrict membership.

Include as much information as you think may be useful. The carp 'grapevine' and the angling press can provide details about fish captures and these can be incorporated, preferably on a map. A picture of the productive areas of the country will soon build up. When talking to fishing acquaintances on the telephone, keep the book to hand and note down any hints they drop about various carp waters. Often, several clues, perhaps from different sources, when put together will solve the riddle. Other sources of information about carp waters are the local meetings and national conferences of the Carp Society and the Carp Anglers' Association. There is also a very useful book, *Guide to Carp Waters*, published by Beekay, which lists 450 waters in all parts of Britain.

A flexible approach

It is important to believe that you have the ability to catch carp. Avoid being envious and remember that the difference between success and failure is often only a little knowledge and some application. If you do not want to put the necessary effort into your fishing, fine, but do not begrudge those that do their rewards. Adopting the same style of fishing under all circumstances, is a recipe for failure. If there is one thing that you must remember, it is to always have a flexible approach. A little friendly competitiveness is harmless and can even be a spur to that extra effort. But sacrificing all for the kudos of catching the most, or the biggest, carp will set you apart all right, but not in the way you expected!

Let me give a simple, but frequently encountered, example of what I mean by 'slipping into a routine' and 'flexible approach'. On many carp waters there are a large number of anglers whose approach to carp fishing consists of arriving at the water, erecting a 'bivvy', casting out three rods with 2-oz (60 g) leads and a 'hair-rigged boilie', and catching up on some sleep until they get a 'churner'. This somewhat *laissez-faire* approach catches a fair number of carp with the minimum of effort. Its shortcomings are often shown up, though, by the angler who exploits the full range of carp-fishing methods. So often such an angler will arrive, spend the necessary time searching for his quarry, and then catch one, or two, 'on the top'. All around, the 'bed-chair brigade' bemoan their fortunes compared with the luck of the nonconformist!

Whether or not carp have intelligence is open to question, and largely depends on the criteria used to define intelligence, but what is beyond doubt is that they have the ability to remember, for extensive periods, and learn from their mistakes. It has been shown, moreover, that some fish have insight and apprehension, and the possession of these attributes indicates intelligence.

Carp can be caught by every fishing method imaginable, but the type of water and the extent of fishing pressure, past and present, will determine to a considerable degree the success of specific methods. You can catch carp on surface baits, on baits fished hard on the bottom, and at any depth in between. Baits attached to a float, baits attached to a weight, and baits attached to nothing but a hook will all catch carp. Not so many years ago it was usual to fish a bottom bait by free-lining. All that was attached to the line was the hook and bait. This obviously limits considerably the distance that the bait can be cast, but, even so, a great number of carp were caught by this method. The use of water-soluble PVA (polyvinyl alcohol) in carp fishing, which began in the early 1970s, allows a weight (usually a stone or a steel nut) to be attached near the bait to aid casting. As the PVA quickly dissolves and the weight drops off, the rig reverts to a free-line set-up.

Nowadays, free-lining is little used, although it has advantages in certain circumstances. If carp can be seen feeding in the margins or close to the bank, especially if the water is shallow, a simple free-lined bait will cause less disturbance when it enters the water. If carp are feeding, or basking in dense weedbeds, particularly lilies, then a free-line rig has several advantages. The bait will almost certainly have to land close to a fish for it to be aware of it, and apart from the important consideration of creating less disturbance than a weighted line, it will also fall through the water much more slowly, in a natural manner. A further benefit is that, because there is nothing else attached to the line, there is less likelihood of becoming badly snagged up in the weed.

Placing the bait effectively

Never rush to cast a bait to a fish that is in a difficult position, such as in the middle of a lily bed or next to some sunken branches. Take the time to think about the situation carefully. Where is the best position to put the bait to least frighten the carp and yet give you a reasonable chance of retrieving it if the fish shows no interest? If the carp takes the bait, can it be landed, or would another vantage point be preferable? Will the tackle be strong enough to do the job? Would it be wiser to first ask a friend to keep alert in case you need assistance? Work out exactly what you think is going to happen and then plan accordingly. In situations such as this the action will be explosive, leaving you no time to change your mind.

It is sometimes necessary to go into the water to land a fish that has become completely snagged up. Do not do so unless you are an accomplished swimmer. If weed and silt make swimming difficult, but the lack of depth makes wading to the fish possible, tie a rope (floating polypropylene is ideal) around your waist and fasten the end to something immovable on the bank. If you do get into difficulties, by sinking too deep into the silt, for example, then at least you can pull yourself out. Such an incident may not happen very often, but once is enough to be fatal, and no carp, no matter how big, is worth risking your life for.

The modern carp angler seems to have little interest in float fishing, which is a shame because it is probably the most aesthetically enjoyable method available to the consummate carp angler. As the great B.B. so admirably puts it, 'It is no surprise when the scarlet quill, which for so long has been resting quietly, a perching place for dragonflies, begins to quiver oh, so slightly . . .' For presentation and bite indication with small baits such as maggots, float fishing is unbeatable. Unfortunately, however, it has one serious flaw. In clear water the line rising from the bottom can be seen, and ultimately carp may associate this with danger.

This major drawback was amply demonstrated to me when I fished the delightful lake at Cave Castle in Yorkshire. It was usual to find the carp 'bubbling' on the shallows of this ancient, silted-up estate lake from early to mid-morning in high summer. They seemed to work at random, rooting in the sediment here and there for their secret food. Since it appeared that luck was all that allowed them to find the bait when they were feeding in this manner, to increase the odds, three or four small, separate areas were quite heavily baited with maggots. After a while one of the carp would chance across the free offerings and root about for more.

John Dennis float-fished maggots to take this fine brace of carp.

A simple rig was all that was needed, with the shot bunched around the float and a size 6 or 8 hook holding half a dozen maggots. This rig was over-cast, well past the fish, and gently drawn back until it was above it, where it was allowed to gently sink to the bottom. If the bite was not immediate, it did not usually take long! But then first an odd fish, then more and more, would suddenly bolt as if startled. A change to ledgered maggots, with enough slack line to ensure that the business end was lying well on the bottom, proved that it was the visibility of the line which was causing the problem.

Occasionally, carp appear to behave in strange ways. For one season, on a popular day-ticket fishery in North Humberside, the majority of the carp were caught by fishing a 'boilie' suspended 2 ft (0.6 m) below a float, over water 10–15 ft (3–4.5 m) deep. Most unnatural, but the carp seemed to prefer it to baits fished on or near the bottom, or to floating baits.

Fishing in coloured water

Coloured water is generally caused by algal blooms, which turn the water green and are often associated with rich waters; or by an abundance of suspended silt particles, indicating a 'hungry' water in which too many fish are continually sifting through the sediment in search of food items; or, sometimes, by a sudden influx of water from a flooded stream. Carp will often feed right in the margins in coloured water, their presence betrayed to the observant by perhaps the tip of the tail breaking the surface, by an occasional ripple or eddy, or sometimes simply by the twitch of a reed stem.

If the carp remains feeding in one area there should be no problem in gently lowering a float-fished bait near it. If the fish is working along the margin, then there is a reasonable chance that its route can be plotted. It seems appropriate in these situations, although there are no valid reasons for assuming so, to use 'natural' baits such as worms, maggots, casters or slugs. Although few carp anglers ever take advantage of the fact, carp often feed right in the margins at night, particularly in clear waters that have a lot of daytime bankside activity. It is tremendously exhilarating to sit, cross-legged, on the edge of the bank in the middle of the night, trying to imperceptibly lower a bait to a big carp which is feverishly feeding at your feet, watching in the pale moonlight its head silently break the surface as it grubs among the roots of the bankside vegetation. That is far, far more exciting than being fast asleep on a bed-chair!

In the early days of carp fishing it was accepted that the hook should be buried in the bait, with at most just the point showing. While baits remained relatively soft, it was possible to pull the hook through the bait on the strike and so hook the carp. With the advent of 'boilies', with their tough skin which deters the attentions of other species, it became necessary to leave a large part of the hook protruding from the bait. Since the bend on a small hook would leave the point barely proud of the bait, large hooks (size 2) are normally used. This has become known as 'side mounting' (see diagram below) and was really the forerunner of the self-hooking rigs currently used.

The next development was the 'bolt rig', in which the bait is mounted on the eye of the hook and is used in conjunction with a short hook link and a heavy lead. The lead can be free-running, or fixed, but the line needs to be held tight with a clip. Takes, when they come, should be instantaneous, so double-check that nothing untoward can happen, otherwise the rod might suddenly disappear into the lake. If takes are resulting in the line just being pulled out of the clip, and the hook is not being set, then often a small adjustment in the length of the hook link, or making absolutely sure that the hook is proud of the bait, will bring success. This principle can be applied to any bait, such as worm, maggots, beans and seeds, which can be mounted on the hook in a similar fashion.

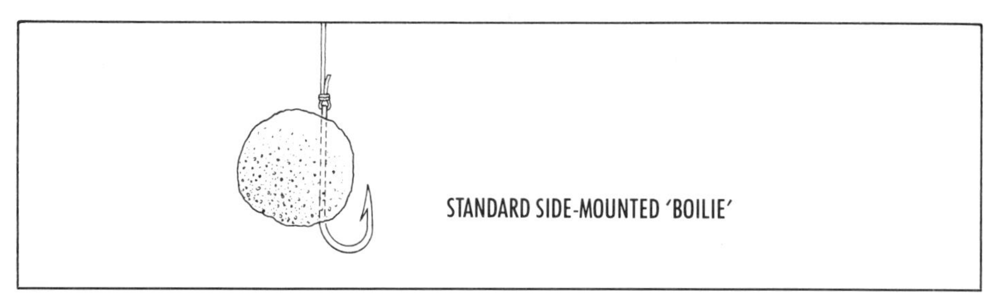
STANDARD SIDE-MOUNTED 'BOILIE'

The 'hair rig'

The history of carp fishing has shown that whatever 'ultimate' rig or bait is developed, it is not long before the fish are a match for it. Thus the heady period of success is followed by a time of consolidation and book writing. Then someone comes up with a truly revolutionary idea which has the carp fooled . . . for a while. Such a concept was the 'hair rig', devised by Lenny Middleton and Kevin Maddocks. They carried out a number of experiments on carp held in a large aquarium at Kevin's home. It soon became apparent that the carp would not pick up any bait which was presented on a line, although unattached offerings were readily accepted.

Lenny and Kevin spent the whole of the winter of 1978 trying out various ideas which they hoped would circumvent the association in the carp's mind of line with danger. Finally, Lenny came up with the suggestion of keeping the bait separate from the hook but attached to it by something which was fine enough to be undetectable by the carp and which would also allow the bait to behave in an identical manner to the free offerings. Their initial trials were carried out using human hair – hence 'hair rig' – but this was soon replaced by fine nylon line. They managed to keep the reason for their resulting success a secret for an amazing amount of time, but eventually it became public knowledge.

While not in the least wishing to detract from Kevin and Lenny's innovative work and the results of their aquarium tests, I have to say that it is now generally accepted that the reasons for the universal success of their idea have not so much to do with the thinness, or undetectability of the hair, but more with the way in which carp repeatedly suck in and blow out food. Clearly, if the hook is actually in the bait, and especially if the bait is fairly buoyant, the weight of the hook will make the bait behave differently from the free offerings. However, it is difficult to believe that a carp has the ability to detect any difference in the behaviour of the bait if it is attached to a 'hair' of 10 lb (4.5 kg) breaking-strain nylon rather than to 1 lb (0.45 kg) nylon. The difference in weight of 1 in (2.5 cm) lengths of

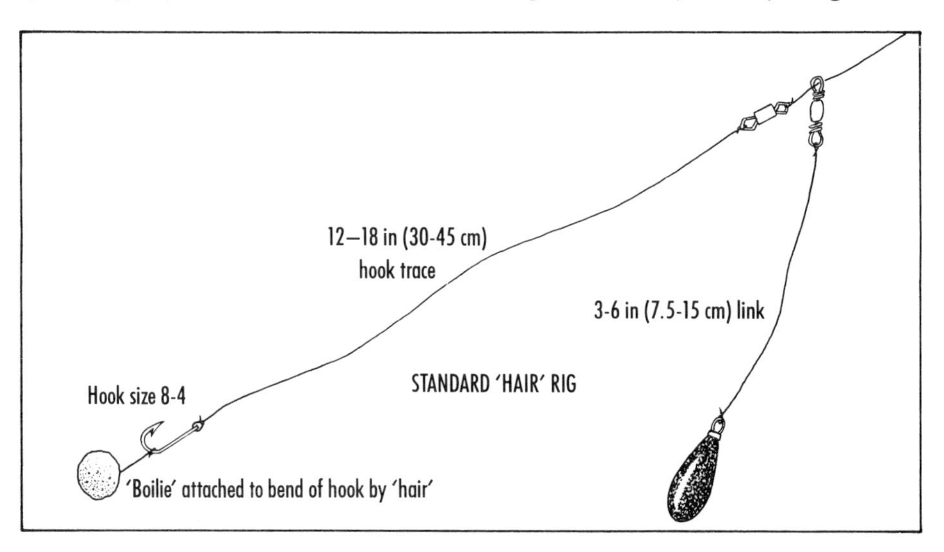

STANDARD 'HAIR' RIG

these two different-strength lines would be negligible. There may be a slight difference in the behaviour of the bait due to the stiffness of the heavier line, but this should not be particularly significant except, perhaps, on heavily fished waters.

Since there is nothing to lose by using thin and/or very supple material for the 'hair', the majority of carp anglers nowadays tend to use either fine nylon, Dacron or dental floss. Although nylon can be quite satisfactory when used for hook links, most anglers believe that more supple materials are advantageous, and braided lines, made from Dacron and Terylene, dental floss and Kryston Multi-Strand, are generally used.

There have been many variations on the original 'hair rig' concept. Some have had merit but many lack any advantage whatsoever. The vast majority of carp have been, and still are, caught on what really is the basic 'hair rig' (see diagram opposite). This is not to say that there have been no developments in this area. There have been, for example, advances in buoyant baits, floating baits, 'stringers' and related tackle.

Bait presentation

Let us look in a simple straightforward way at why we get bites. When you have a problem, it usually pays to strip it down to basics in order to understand what is going on. Before you can hook a carp, there are two main factors that you have to get right. First, you have to have a bait that, at the very least, the carp are not going to either ignore or be frightened of. A good bait will come with knowledge, experience, luck, maybe a stroke of genius, but mainly through trial and error.

Secondly, you have to do your utmost to ensure that the carp do not suspect there is anything unnatural in the behaviour of the bait. Generally, this means they should not be able to differentiate between the behaviour of the hook bait and any identical free offerings. One way of achieving this is simply to not provide any free offerings, and there have been plenty of carp caught by anglers just casting out a single 'boilie'. The problem with this is that the carp may take a long time to come across an individual bait, although it is not such a bad idea if you know carp regularly frequent a particular area. Making the bait highly visible, for example by making it buoyant and fishing it well off the bottom, as shown in the diagram below, can help in this situation.

Another way is to use free offerings that differ substantially from that used on the hook. A lot of success has been achieved in recent years by fishing a 'boilie' on the hook over a bed of particles, including mixtures of hemp seed, maize, tiger nuts, and peanuts. Most anglers, when preparing their own 'boilies', tend to try and make them of an identical size. There are no benefits in doing this, and in fact there is an advantage in doing just the opposite. When 'boilies' vary in size they behave differently in the water, making it less likely that the carp will be able to distinguish the hook bait from the free offerings.

The hook's efficiency

Since the hook has an important relationship to the bait, and is the means by which the fish is attached to the angler, the way in which it performs makes the difference between success and failure. A hook's efficiency is always a question of compromise. Increase the thickness of the wire and you increase the strength of the hook, but

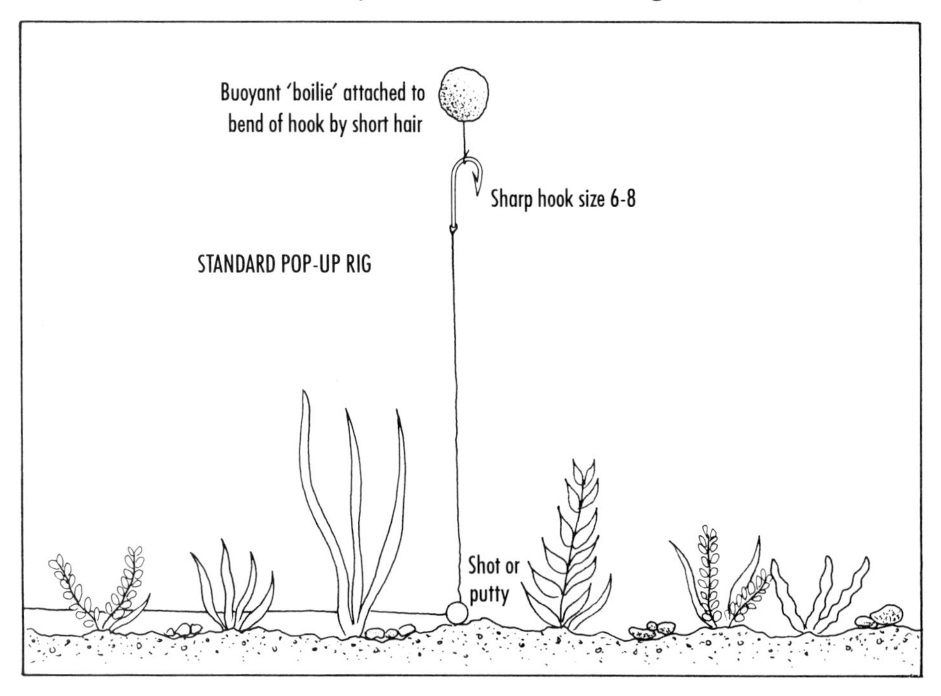

you also increase the weight. A larger hook is less likely to tear free, but a bigger hook will weigh more. The heavier the hook, the more likely it will be to influence the behaviour of the bait and so arouse the suspicions of the fish. Of paramount importance is the hook's sharpness. It used to be the case that the majority of hooks, when purchased, were not sharp enough and they had to be honed with a small file or emery stone. But the recent advances in chemically sharpened hooks have made this unnecessary and because these hooks are so sharp they have become an essential part of the success of the 'hair rig'. Hooks are, to a great extent, a matter of personal preference, but without doubt some are simply better than others. Given the same conditions, some are stronger, have better hooking abilities and are less prone to pulling out. My personal choices are:

1 Open water fishing with 6–8 lb (2.7–3.5 kg) line: Drennan 'Carbon Specimen'
2 Open water/some weed with 8–10 lb (3.5–4.5 kg) line: Drennan 'Super Specialist'
3 Heavy weed/snag fishing with 12–15 lb (5.5–7 kg) line: Au Lion D'Or, 1545

Other respected anglers also recommend hooks which are undoubtedly excellent by Au Lion D'Or, Partridge, Mustad and Rod Hutchinson.

There can be few anglers who would disagree that catching carp 'off the top' is the most exciting of methods. Watching a big carp suspiciously examine the bait, then repeatedly almost take it, only to turn away at the very last moment, can be too much to bear. Chris Ball is an addict, but with enough guile and experience to make him a successful one. His contribution, which follows, gives an insight into an area of carp fishing which perhaps embodies the true spirit of the sport.

'ON THE TOP' BY CHRIS BALL

Any carp angler who has either caught sight of, or studied at length, big carp at close range, knows what an awe-inspiring sight is one of those superb creatures going about its business. Always cautious, but always inquisitive, the carp is equally at home searching the bottom or investigating odd bits and pieces of food floating on the surface. Many carp anglers will tell you that one of the greatest thrills has to be seeing a carp actually take a hook bait. Unfortunately, not many anglers put themselves in a position to do just that.

The practice of fishing behind two or more rods with 'boilies' or particles has never been more popular, and with just reason, for at times tremendous catches are possible. However, this has led in turn to the vast majority of carp anglers ignoring stalking tactics, in particular on the surface.

I have enjoyed particular success with surface fishing for carp for many years on a good variety of waters, in all kinds of conditions. This is a heart-stopping and unbelievably exciting way of fishing. It all comes down to seeing the fish approach the hook bait and actually take it, often in a most spectacular manner.

Carp can at times become preoccupied with baits such as Chum Mixer, or any of the dog or cat biscuits that float. And it does not have to be a blazing-hot day for this method to be successful, although warm weather does help. You will find that an overcast day, with a strong ripple on the water, can also produce good results. Even in winter I have caught fish of over 10 lb (4.5 kg) – once while ice was on the water.

Baiting tactics

My approach is nearly always to throw out free offerings, then, when the carp are taking these well, to cast to either the biggest fish I can see, or the largest mouth that sticks out of the water. You really can do this, for the carp will be on the top and if they are close enough you can spot them very easily, especially if you can get on higher ground. Where that is not possible, look for the largest mouth, although this is not always reliable as many a 12 lb (5.5 kg) or 14 lb (6.5 kg) carp I have caught had a mouth twice the size of that of a 20 lb (9 kg) fish. Casting to individual fish is possible only when there are numbers of fish 'having the bait'. Competition for food makes them less wary but still some fish will know which baits to avoid. The main problem is the line, either floating or sunk, near the hook bait. Persevere with these difficult carp because you will get one in the end, either because a fish makes a mistake or because it is annoyed by this piece of food constantly appearing in front of it. You must put the hook bait in the path you think the fish will be travelling, *not* on top of its head each time. In fact you will not get more than one chance if you do the latter.

Anchoring the bait out in open water with the line coming up from a bomb is a successful method but the carp will get wise to this, for again the problem is the fish feeling the line just at the last moment. This difficulty with the line in surface fishing has been countered with ingenuity by anglers and manufacturers alike. Their efforts have spawned such solutions as the beachcaster rig and the 'Suspender' float. Both set-ups rely on the fact that no line touches the water in the vicinity of the floating hook bait, and they do work. On the first occasion I tried the Gardner 'Suspender' it produced seven fish in an afternoon's fishing. Until I used it these fish were just swirling at the hook bait in a very frustrating manner. They took some time to figure out what was happening but ultimately my chances again became few and far between.

One method that has many of the advantages that I have mentioned, but is rarely practised, is 'margin fishing'. Richard Walker found out years ago that carp, especially after dark, would patrol the margins where there was enough depth and would succumb to a crust lowered directly beneath the rod tip. No line touches the water to scare them and it can be of any strength you choose. I use this method in the daytime, for if you are quiet enough in your approach, or you are already in position waiting for the fish, you can literally lower the bait into a carp's mouth. At a few of the lakes I do this from up a tree – it is always very exciting, because you can see the fish you are after. It is best to use a short little stalking rod for this kind of fishing. Mine is an old 9 ft (275 cm) glass-fibre model with a 'through action'. It seems equally at home hurling out 1 oz (25 g) controllers on 6 lb (2.7 kg) breaking-strain line as it does with 15 lb (7 kg) line under the rod tip.

I have gone over to split-cane rods for open-water fishing. These rods I have restored to their former glory. They are a couple of Bob Southall Mk IVs built in the 1950s and a beautiful old Richard Walker, B. James Mk IV Avon. It will be thrilling to catch a 30 lb (14 kg) carp on one of these. They are robust enough for the job and add a nice, nostalgic touch to my surface fishing.

Surface-fishing waters

After that brief round-up of some of the methods I have found successful for catching carp 'off the top', let us look at the kinds of waters involved and the carp's reaction to surface food. I have found over many years that there is not one water which I have seriously fished where the carp could not be persuaded to take a surface bait. This has applied to waters from the overstocked, easy kind right through to the most difficult lakes. However, when I say there is not one water that has not responded, getting carp to feed in the close season is entirely different from when you actually start to fish for them. A prime example is the Match Lake at Yateley which forms part of the Leisure Sport Angling complex. Here I have tried, on and off, for ten years to get a carp 'off the top'. They show absolutely no interest, even in ideal conditions.

Only once, some years ago, in late April, did they show any interest. A considerable number of fish were shoaled up in the far bay. I catapulted out some Chum Mixer to drift down towards them and, although they were cautious at first, after a short time they went totally mad! I thought to myself that I had to get one finally. Yet that one instance is the only time they ever fed like that in open water, and I really tried. I admit that I am baffled by this. In the end the only way I *could* catch them was in the lily pads, by just dangling Chum from the end of the rod tip. In this area of the lake carp would hole up on most warm days and I could, after a while, get them to take free offerings. But I did notice that the offerings they took were not between the lily pads themselves, but in holes in the leaves. You can often see these holes appear from late July onwards as the pads become tatty.

Other lakes that have on occasion produced good catches can become comparatively easy if you can stay one step ahead of the fish as far as presentation is concerned. One memorable period at a water in Surrey saw the carp inspect every piece of Chum and only take those that they found were safe. But the split second when the hook bait was inspected, when they closed their extendable top lip over it, was the time I struck, before the bait was refused. Very sneaky, but it worked.

I hope these examples will show that you have to be versatile, as with all methods of carp fishing. Just chucking out a piece of floating

A large carp being played with skill and patience. Overhead pressure has brought the fish to the surface.

Linda Tyree nets a fine fish, weed and all.

A massive north-west carp. It is unusual for such a large fish to be found in the north of England.

A carp angler's dream – a 30 lb 4 oz (13 kg) leather carp, caught on a float-fished boilie.

This carp from Stamps Pond fell to Les Munday's floating bait during the middle of the day. Heavy weed made strong tackle necessary.

crust when the weather is warm and a few carp are moving around on top will only bring limited success. Probably one of the most difficult challenges in 'floater' fishing is to tackle a large water with very few carp present. The following story tells how I managed to catch a 'whopper' from such a water by careful observation, and some luck, over a period of time. Wraysbury Lake in Middlesex has the reputation of being one of the most difficult waters in the country, mainly because there are so few carp in its vast expanse. To see one may be regarded as an event, and the anglers who have caught a Wraysbury carp can almost be counted on two hands! I knew from some of my friends that carp could be tempted 'on the top' if you could only find them. Wraysbury is a lake that has so many nooks and crannies, small bays, headlands and back channels, that the carp can hide away unnoticed by all except those fortunate enough to have the time to continually search them out.

Wraysbury challenge

In the close season of 1987 I started to visit Wraysbury when the weather improved, towards the end of April. Although I spent a fair amount of time just looking in likely areas, it was not until some really hot weather came that I found a fish. Just one, under an overhanging bush. It was a good fish, very dark, broad and deep. I wanted to find out its reaction to Chum so I threw some out on the far side of the bush to drift in, but before the fish had a chance to find any of the bait, it was pounced upon by two others which I had not noticed. The carp from under the bush came out to join in, and for a long time that afternoon I fed those fish. It was encouraging, to say the least. I told one of the regular anglers about this event, and he thought that they were carp which had been put in the lake only a couple of years before. He believed that kind of response from true Wraysbury fish was unlikely. I was disappointed at first, then I reasoned that if these three fish were in among some of the other Wraysbury carp one day, and I managed to get them feeding, there would be a chance that some of the others might join in.

One afternoon not long after, I found the 'whoppers' again and they took Chum just as readily as on the previous occasion. But for the fact that it was during the close season, the prospects were looking better all the time. I did manage to catch three fish 'on the top' that season, and I felt satisfied with my efforts. The one problem I was faced with was, I never got close to or found any of the really big carp. The three I did catch were good fish but I knew there were carp at least 15 lb (7 kg) heavier somewhere out there.

A renewed campaign

The 1988 season found me more determined than ever as I started a campaign against the Wraysbury leviathans. The weather, which had been very hot immediately before the start of the season, changed to cloudy but rather humid. In the first few hours of the season I came close to catching a carp on a bottom-fished bait, in a snaggy area of the lake where I found four fish. But these never returned and, during the next two days, they did a 'Houdini' act. I went round the whole lake several times looking for them, sometimes taking the whole day. I never cast once.

On 20 June I arrived again at Wraysbury. The weather was very sticky and I wondered if I would find those carp that day. Hours later I had given up and was walking back to the car to leave when something made me turn around and look out into the lake. From where I stood I could see way out to some islands. I looked, blinked and looked again. In the far distance there were some huge bow waves which were reasonably close to the left-hand bank, about a quarter of a mile (0.4 km) from where I was. I flew to the car and, carefully tackling up the little stalking rod, shot back to the lake.

When I arrived at the spot the group of fish had swum further along the bank, so I picked my tackle up and moved. As I walked along I could see that they were turning, so I quickly moved back to my original position. Out went a couple of pouch-loads of Chum Mixer, which landed about 20 yd (18 m) out but, with the wind, quickly drifted towards some fish. There was a swirl, but I could not see if the carp had taken some bait or had bolted! Then I had a stroke of luck you require at times like this. Suddenly the wind died and it went quite calm and four different fish appeared very much closer to the bank: I fired some more Chum out and these fish went crazy. They were fighting each other for it. One fish in particular showed its huge, creamy white belly each time it took a free offering. It was obviously a 'whopper', and this was the one I had to catch.

A day to remember

As these four fish swirled at the Chum it became dissipated and the big one became detached from the others. I cast out to a spot 20 ft (6 m) ahead of the fish and, as it approached the hook-bait, it accelerated and took the bait on the run. As the line jerked tight and I struck, there was a tremendous swirl and water shot up into the air. I was using a light line but there were no snags anywhere near, so I knew I stood a good chance of landing it. As with many big carp, it fought with that slow, solid pressure, and after quite some time I managed to get it into the margins, which were deep and clear of obstructions. That tremendous bulk, with a small head and massive shoulder, chugged up and down for a long time. Several times I tried to get it ready for the net, but each time it bore away strongly. The line pinging across the fish's back every now and then had my heart in my mouth. But in the net it finally went and I punched the air! It was certainly a terrific experience, and what carp fishing is really all about. The fish was a monster all right, and a little later, with help from some friends, I weighed it accurately. A magnificent mirror carp, it weighed 36¼ lb (16.5 kg) and was 33 in (84 cm) to the fork of the tail, with a girth of 32½ in (83 cm). My first 30 lb-plus (14 kg) carp on a 'floater' and a Wraysbury fish as well. It was a day I shall always remember.

PREBAITING

Prebaiting is, without doubt, one of the most useful and misunderstood techniques. It is often claimed that heavy prebaiting can ruin sport by overfeeding, but this is unlikely unless taken to extremes. In carp, the digestion of food takes place as it travels through the intestine. If the fish takes a surfeit of food, the freshly ingested food causes that which is already in the intestine to be excreted before it is fully digested. Although the carp does not have a true stomach like that of a pike or trout, it can eat considerable quantities of food over short periods. I have known carp increase their body weight by 10 per cent within a few hours by feeding on anglers' bait. So it is quite feasible for half a dozen large carp to consume up to 12 lb (5.5 kg) of bait overnight. And the higher the water temperature, the faster the food will be digested.

Prebaiting achieves several goals. It allows carp to recognize a new type of bait. The time it takes for the carp to accept the bait depends, to a large extent, upon the bait itself, and also on the past experience of the fish. Some baits are pretty instant – for example, sweetcorn – whereas others take time. Prebaiting can also encourage carp to feed in certain areas, and to feed on a particular bait, with a sense of security. But it will not, ultimately, ensure that you will catch more fish from a particular water. What is more likely is that it will speed up the process, often resulting in the capture of fish in numbers.

It is best to prebait after dark. This reduces the chances of unscrupulous characters seeing where you are baiting and later moving in and reaping the benefits of your efforts. Furthermore, on many waters certain water birds, mainly coots and tufted ducks, are a considerable nuisance. They are fully aware that a man on the bank, using a catapult, fires little balls of food into the water for them!

The amount of bait introduced, the period over which prebaiting is carried out, and the time between introductions are all difficult to quantify as they depend on many variables. However, in the case of a reasonably stocked carp water, I would plan to introduce a new bait over two or three weeks, putting in perhaps 200 'boilies' every other night. If fewer trips were possible, perhaps because of distance, then I would certainly introduce the same amount of bait, but spread it over a wider area to begin with, then confine it to the intended swim over the last two or three trips. I would also incorporate a particle bait into the prebaiting for these final few trips.

It has become fashionable nowadays to put out markers to identify the prebaited swim. The problem with this is that it also identifies it for other carp anglers. Unless you fish a water where all the anglers respect an individual's efforts, do not advertise!

Introducing the bait

Partly because I prefer to introduce bait after dark I have a wide range of catapults which will fire it out to different set distances. After deciding on a particular swim during a daylight 'sortie', I choose the appropriate catapult for the job. A mark on the opposite bank, a tree, or a telegraph pole or pylon which will stand out against the skyline at night, is used as a direction finder. I select a weight of the size required for casting out to the baited area and use a line marker to confirm this distance. The importance of putting your hook bait in exactly the same area as the groundbait cannot be overstated. A few yards can make all the difference. A classic example of this involved a couple of well-known carp anglers, whose names I will refrain from mentioning, who were fishing the notoriously difficult Savay Lake in the Colne Valley. They were fishing the same swim, but one angler was catching the majority of the fish (which were very large). They had baited an area where they knew the fish were, which was at a considerable distance from the bank, but one angler could reach the baited area, while the other was consistently falling a few yards short.

It is difficult to judge how much bait to put in during an actual fishing session. Too much and you can ruin your chances; too little and you might only scratch the surface of the swim's potential. In most circumstances it probably pays to err on the conservative side. It is always possible to put a bit more in, but if you overdo it at the start there is no way of getting it out again! With decisions of this nature it really comes down to a gut feeling based on experience. But a bit of 'fishy' logic does not go amiss.

Consider the example of a single, all-night session. You do not know how many carp are in the swim. Therefore, what is the maximum amount of bait you can put out that will still give you a reasonable chance if there is only one fish in the area? Suppose that at the start of the session you introduce a hundred 'freebies' and use two rods. The chances of a fish picking up the hook bait straight away would be pretty remote. So if you do get a bite early in the session, either you have been very fortunate or, more likely, there are several fish picking up the bait. Using this line of reasoning, a rough rule of thumb would indicate that if you get a take fairly early on, 50 per cent of the bait has already gone. At that point I would fire out a further twenty-five to fifty 'boilies' and would continue introducing that sort of quantity of bait as long as I was getting bites.

Prebaiting will also prolong the life of a bait. The more free offerings a fish is allowed to eat, the less likely it will be to associate danger with that bait after it has been caught on it. This is an important factor concerning the life-span of a bait, but there are also other considerations. Very distinctive flavours and colours in baits tend to make them instantly attractive, but their effect tends to be short-lived. More subtle flavours and less obtrusive colours generally increase the life-span of the bait.

The constituents of some baits may initiate a direct feeding response similar to that experienced by humans. Certain smells and tastes which are attractive to humans have been used extensively in the food industry, particularly in confectionery and snacks. In the 1970s Norfolk's Dick Weale and Len Bunn experimented with various amino acids, basing their investigations on work carried out by the Lowestoft Fishery Research Centre. Undoubtedly, some amino acids have biologically significant scents that can trigger food-searching and feeding responses, but it is probable that specific

When a carp finds the sanctuary of a lily bed, constant pressure may shift it. If not, slackening off completely may work.

mixtures of several compounds, rather than single chemicals, are the key. This line of research is so complicated that it is really beyond the scope of the ordinary carp angler, for it requires sophisticated laboratory techniques. Furthermore, there are potential dangers to fish in exposing them to high doses of pure chemicals whose effects are not, as yet, fully understood.

Alternative baiting techniques

An ideal way of introducing bait in many circumstances is to use a small inflatable boat. A marker float is normally used with this method to ensure that the bait goes *exactly* where it is wanted. Although some fisheries do not allow boats – and this is understandable as their use may result in unreasonable behaviour that ruins other anglers' chances – if they are used with care they do not usually disturb the fish, even in fairly shallow water. A refinement on the use of a boat is to row out the hook baits as well, dropping them directly on top of the groundbait.

Another tactic is to use radio-controlled boats which carry out and release small quantities of bait. To some anglers these methods raise questions of ethics, since they suggest an unsportsmanlike 'the end justifies the means' attitude.

PLAYING BIG CARP

To play and land any fish successfully, you must have tackle which will give you some control over it, whatever the situation. A big carp can accelerate very fast, reaching speeds of about 20 mph (32 km/hr) and causing the spool of a fixed-spool reel to rotate at 60 revolutions per second. You must know exactly what you intend to do once the carp is hooked, because a fish which can travel 10 yards (9 m) in a second can reach the sanctuary of a weedbed or a snag before you have time to decide.

Line strength is often a question of compromise. Strong, thick line allows you to apply more pressure to a hooked fish, but its greater visibility naturally tends to reduce the number of bites. In some cases you will have room to allow the fish to run and take a lot of line from the spool, and then a lighter line of, say, 7–8 lb (3–3·5 kg) breaking strain may be used. You may be fishing 60 yards (55 m)

The author bends into a good fish, applying sidestrain to prevent it reaching a snag. Note the sunken landing net ready for use.

from the bank and it is not unusual in these circumstances for a fish to run 40 yards (35 m). The reel should therefore hold about 150 yards (140 m) of line. In open water the main danger is represented by bottom weed. It may appear fairly sparse but if a fish makes a long run along the bottom, the lead can sometimes accumulate a lot of troublesome weed.

Overhead pressure

When the fish is first hooked, apply pressure by holding the rod vertically overhead. This tends to pull the fish up off the bottom away from the rooted weed. If the fish decides to make a run for a snag, or the safety of a dense weedbed, sidestrain offers the best means of turning it. The rod is held low, with the tip close to the water, and is bent to offer maximum resistance. Few carp can carry on taking line against the combination of reliable tackle and the pressure of sidestrain. However, this tactic tends to cause the fish to 'kite' towards the bank. Then, with the fish heading towards the

It is important to keep your composure when you have hooked a carp. Rehearsing tactics mentally beforehand can help you stay cool.

margins, often at a considerable distance along the bank, you find that the more you pull, the more you are helping it. Snags may be lurking in the marginal vegetation, so the best approach, if feasible, is to make your way along the bank until you are near to the fish, while at the same time keeping pressure on it with the rod upright. Sometimes it is not possible to move along the bank because of trees. The only recourse is to try to get the rod as far out from the bank as possible, perhaps by wading into the margins. Then, holding the rod tip underwater, apply as much pressure as you dare, trying to recover line as quickly as possible and bringing the fish towards you.

Sometimes it is necessary to fish in situations where 'strong-arm' tactics are required. If, for example, you are fishing close to snags or lily beds, the carp must be stopped almost immediately before it

There is no room for the slightest mistake as Len Arbery does battle with one of Redmire Pool's justly famous common carp.

gathers momentum. You have to be constantly alert and heavy pressure must be exerted on the fish as soon as it is hooked. Substantial tackle is clearly required: a line of 12–15 lb (5·5–7 kg) and rods with 2–2½ lb (0·9–1·1 kg) test curve. The reel clutch should be screwed down tight and if a little line has to be given this should be done by allowing the reel to back-wind. It is critical that the catch which stops the reel from backwinding is not engaged. Many anglers prefer to play their fish by backwinding, even though the slipping clutch is specifically designed to allow line to be given. If you decide to use the clutch to give line, then regularly check the tension, as it does vary with changes in temperature. A common fault is to set the clutch far too lightly: line should only start to be given by a strong pull. When you operate the slipping clutch, it is advisable to hold your finger against the spool to increase the drag.

The gearing in reels does not allow you wind a big fish in directly, even if it is not pulling. The only way to gain line is by 'pumping'. The rod is gradually raised till it is vertical, or even slightly over the shoulder, and then the reel is quickly wound in as the rod is lowered to the horizontal. The rod is immediately raised, putting pressure on the fish again, and then slowly moved towards the vertical. As the process is repeated, the fish is gradually brought in.

When the fish is close to the bank, it is a good idea to kneel down to play it. If the carp is unaware of your presence, it is less likely to make a last surge for freedom when the hook can all too easily pull out. Once the fish is under the rod tip, and there is no immediate danger, it is often prudent to ease off with the rod pressure if the fish is still strong. Do not panic into trying to force the fish into the landing net. Once the fish is away from danger, time is on your side and steady pressure will eventually tell, even on the biggest fish.

CHAPTER EIGHT

CARP RIGS

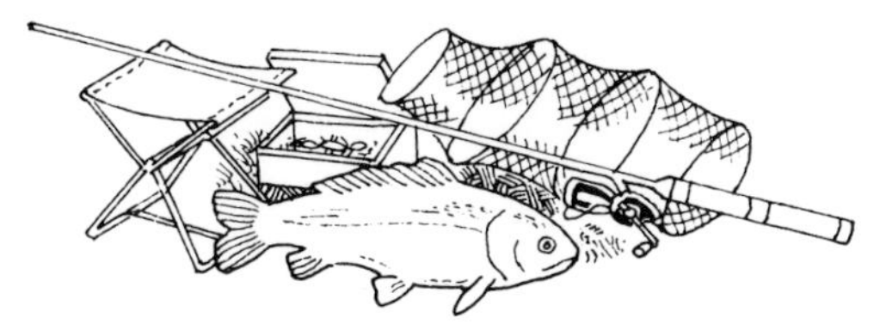

Rigs and set-ups for carp come in all shapes and sizes. Many are publicized as being the latest breakthrough, but in reality the majority have never been anywhere but the drawing board. Few variations of the basic Lenny Middleton–Kevin Maddocks hair-rig (see page 90) have added anything of value, and those that have are only refinements of the original concept. Carp do learn by their mistakes and will gradually 'wise up' to any new bait or rig. The fantastic initial success of the hair-rig has now slowed down considerably and on some waters results are at present no better than those achieved before this innovation came along.

A PROVEN METHOD

The basic rig is nowadays usually fished with either a fixed lead or a 'backstop' (see diagrams on pages 110 and 111). It almost always incorporates a heavy lead, the minimum effective size being 1½–2 oz (40–60 g). When the rig is fished with a tight line, a heavier lead is necessary – usually 2–2½ oz (60–70 g). Although no one is really sure why this type of rig has been so successful, it is generally accepted that since a carp will normally suck in and blow out a bait several times, the free hook has an excellent chance of catching somewhere inside the mouth. When the fish moves away, perhaps realizing something is amiss, it pulls against the lead and its suspicions become reality. The resistance of the lead helps to pull the hook in further and as the fish charges off, the hook is pulled home as the tight line set-up adds further resistance.

Unfortunately, on some heavily pressured waters, the carp now do not charge off when they realize that there is something wrong. They have learnt to stay in the same spot and try and get rid of the

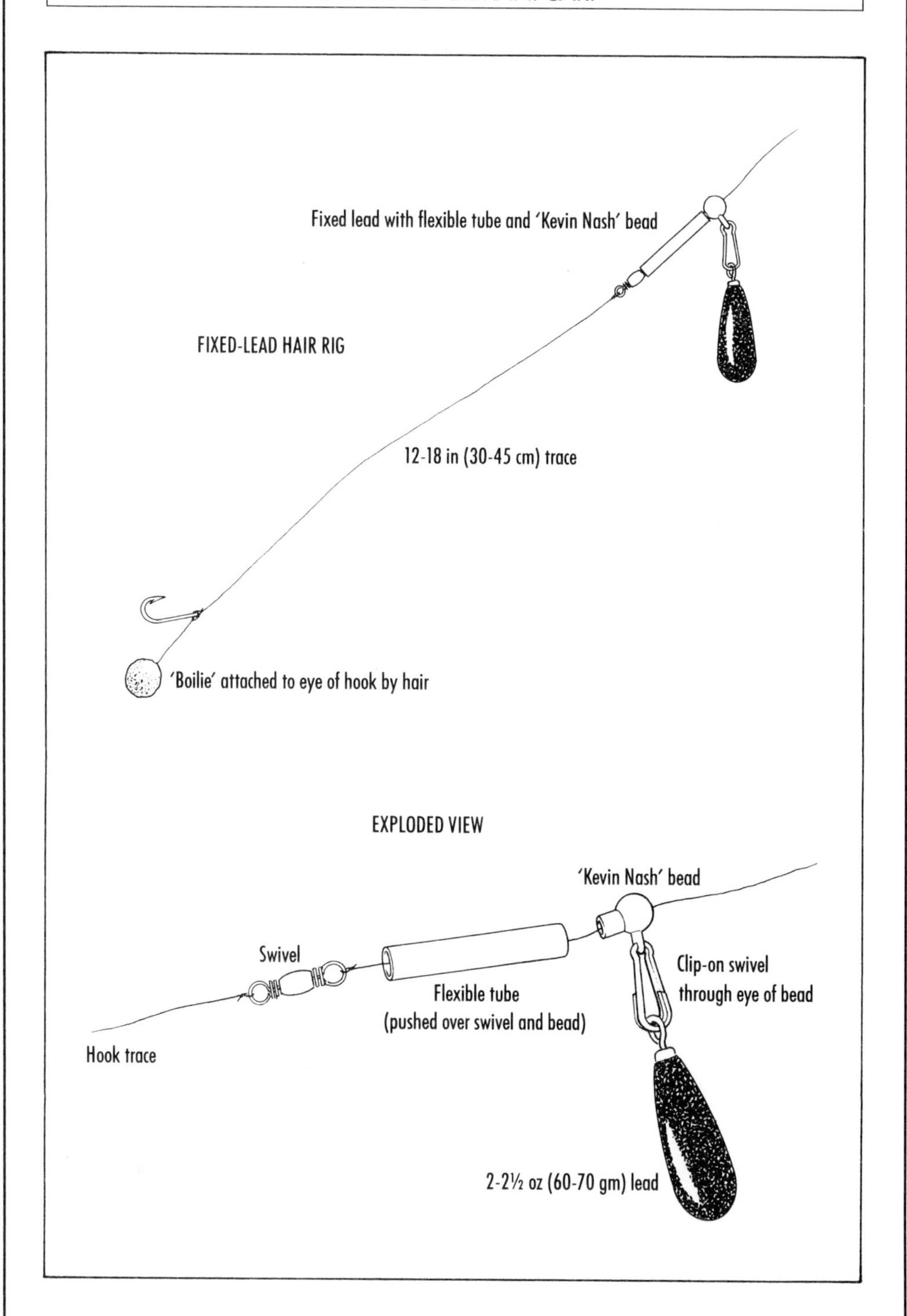
Fixed lead with flexible tube and 'Kevin Nash' bead
FIXED-LEAD HAIR RIG
12-18 in (30-45 cm) trace
'Boilie' attached to eye of hook by hair
EXPLODED VIEW
'Kevin Nash' bead
Swivel
Clip-on swivel
through eye of bead
Flexible tube
(pushed over swivel and bead)
Hook trace
2-2½ oz (60-70 gm) lead

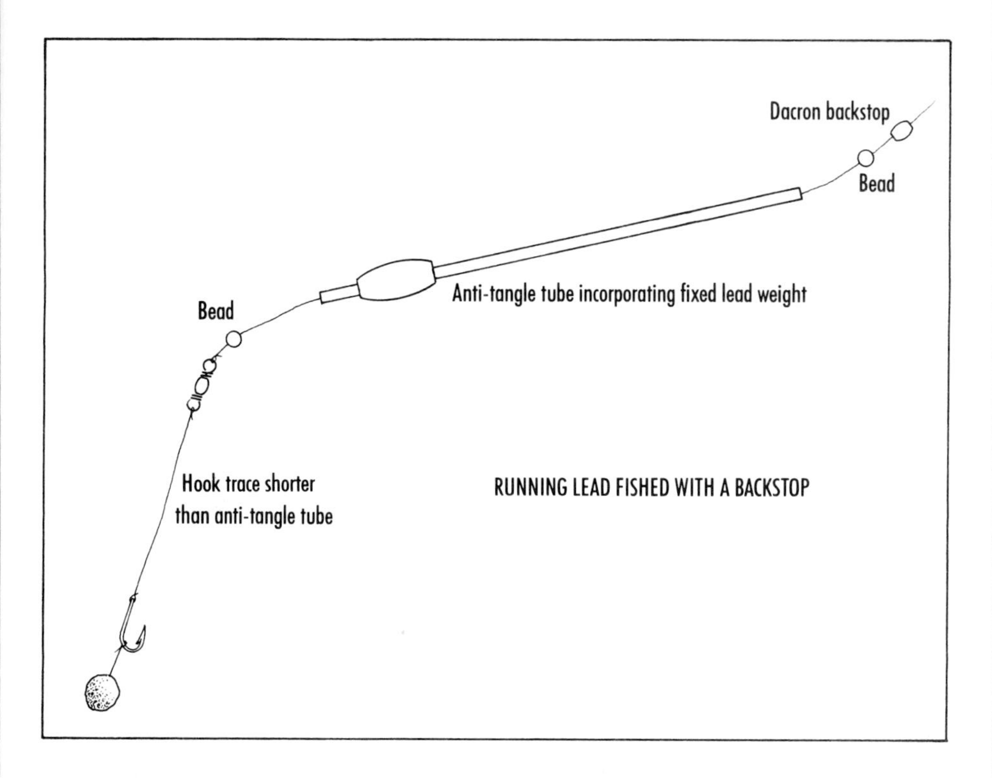

hook. In many cases, if given enough time, they can do this. The only indications are a few twitches, and if this happens in the middle of the night it is all too easy to do nothing! Success takes effort!

On some waters the carp associate the line with danger and here it is necessary to fish with the line lying on the bottom. In these circumstances the tight line set-up cannot be used. It is perhaps even more important when fishing a slack line to use a heavy lead, for it is this alone that has to pull the hook in. Usually, if a couple of yards of line are pulled off the reel, this will ensure enough is lying on the bottom near the bait. But when you are fishing fairly close in, in a lake where the bottom drops off suddenly from the bank, the acute angle thus formed makes it difficult to lay a reasonable amount of line on the lake bed. There is a solution. After the normal procedure of casting out and setting the rod in the rests, a lead of about 2 oz (60 g), with a clip-on swivel, is attached to the line at the rod tip and allowed to slide down the line to the bottom of the lake, pulling the line with it (see diagram on page 112).

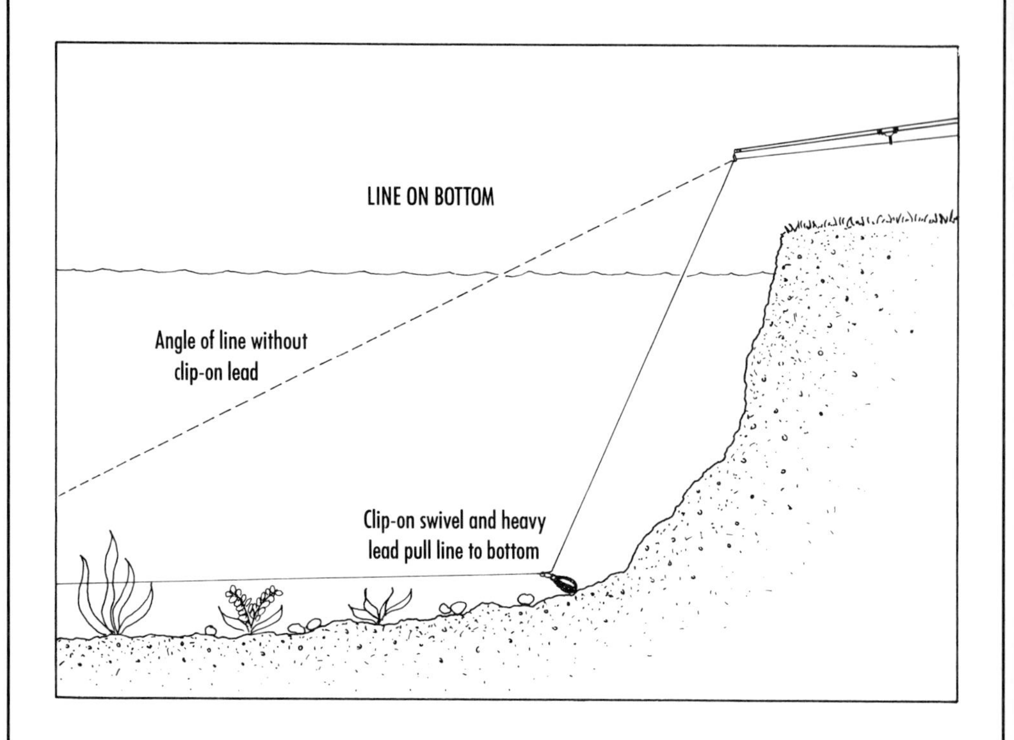

'POP-UPS'

On many waters 'pop-ups' have been very successful. It is usually assumed that their effectiveness is due to the fact that they stand out and are so easily found. Probably the best way of making pop-ups is to cut the 'boilie' in half and remove enough from the inside of each section to allow a small polystyrene ball (available as Polyballs) to be inserted. The two sections can then be rejoined with Superglue. Pop-ups are usually fished 6–18 in (15–45 cm) off the bottom. A swan shot can be set at the required distance from the hook.

When the hair-rig first became widely publicized, hair lengths of 1–1½ in (2.5–4 cm) were recommended. I believe that this is far too long. In most situations the bait's position should vary from just touching the bend of the hook to being no more than ¾ in (2 cm) away (see diagram on page 113). Most other rigs, such as the 'D rig', the sliding rig, the buoyant-hook rig and the anti-ejection rig (see diagrams on pages 113 and 114), are attempts to improve the way in which the hook enters and leaves the carp's mouth.

CARP RIGS

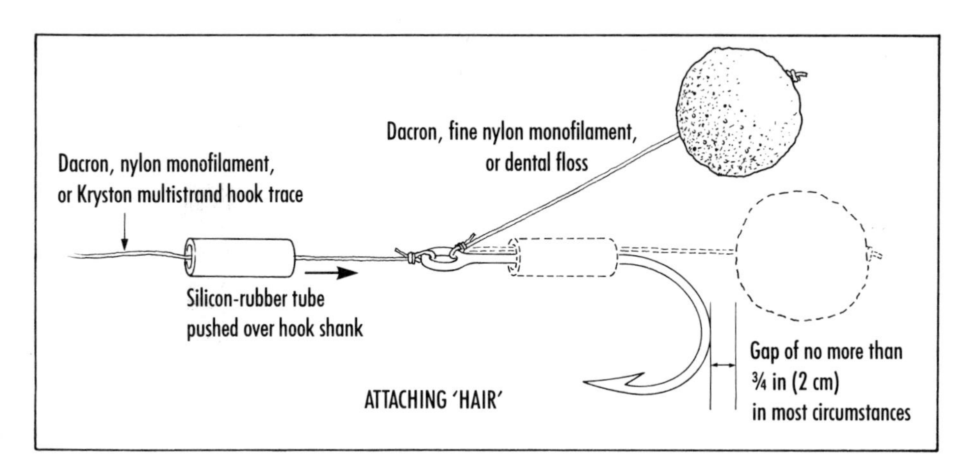
Dacron, fine nylon monofilament,
or dental floss
Dacron, nylon monofilament,
or Kryston multistrand hook trace
Silicon-rubber tube
pushed over hook shank
Gap of no more than
¾ in (2 cm)
in most circumstances
ATTACHING 'HAIR'

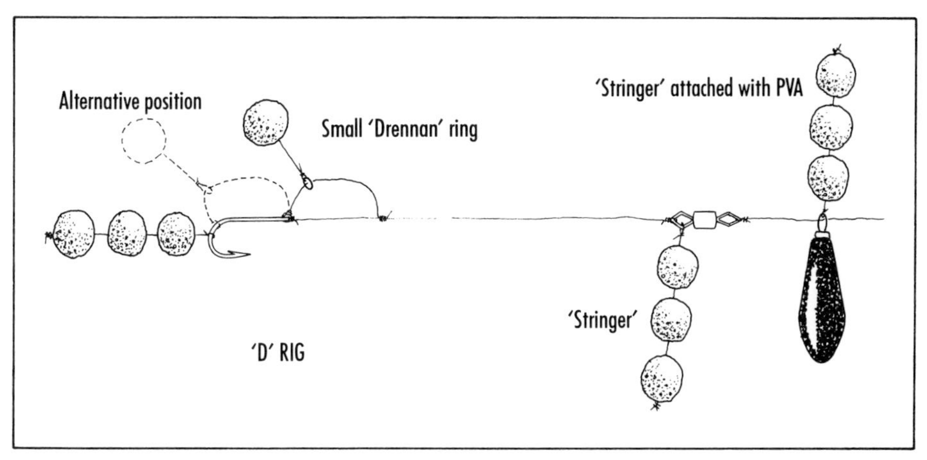
Alternative position
Small 'Drennan' ring
'Stringer' attached with PVA
'Stringer'
'D' RIG

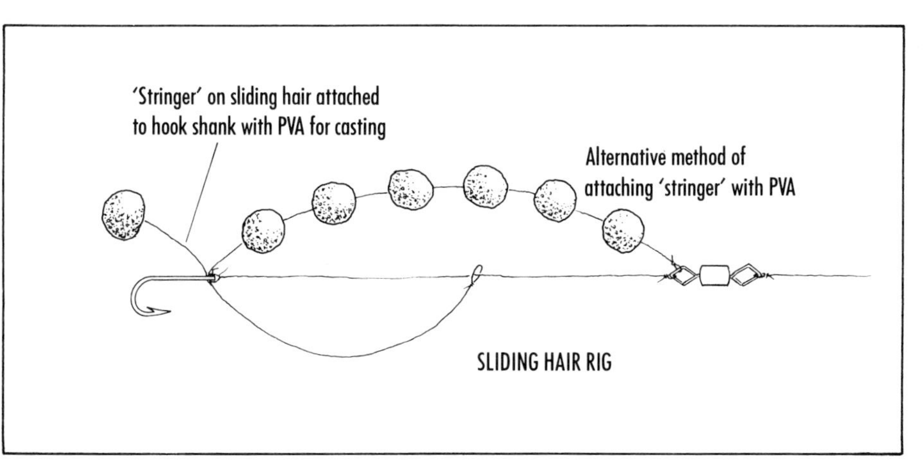
'Stringer' on sliding hair attached
to hook shank with PVA for casting
Alternative method of
attaching 'stringer' with PVA
SLIDING HAIR RIG

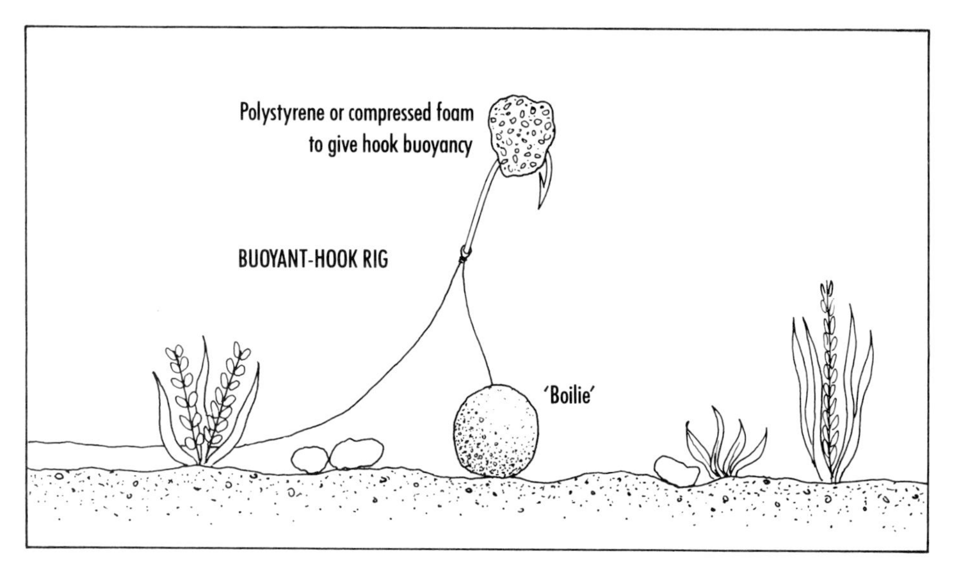
Polystyrene or compressed foam
to give hook buoyancy
BUOYANT-HOOK RIG
'Boilie'

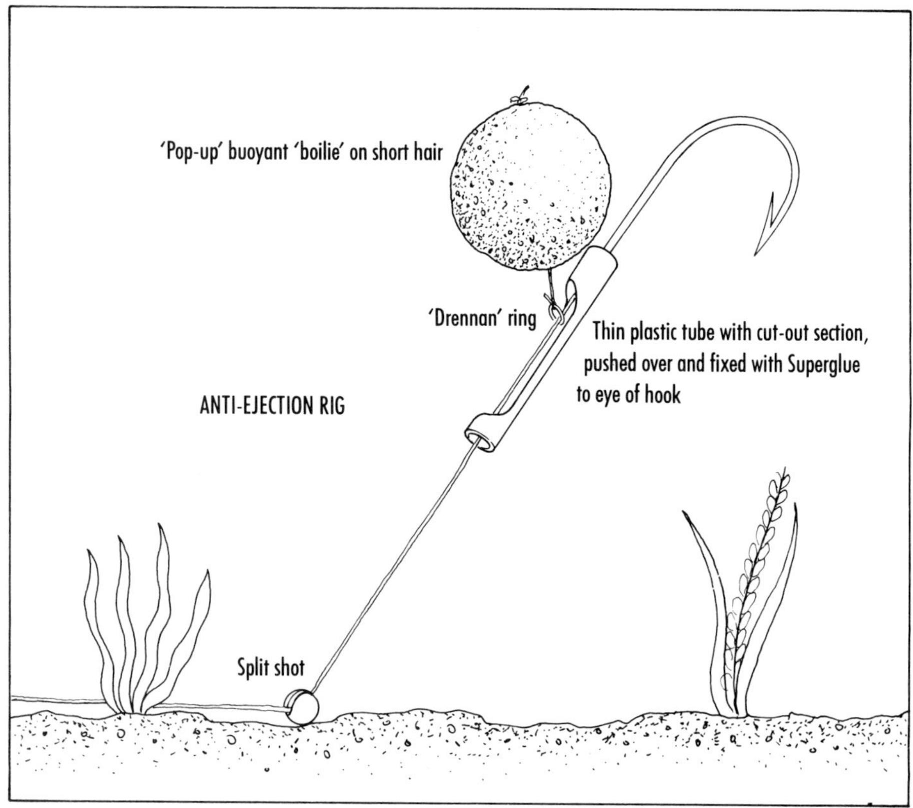
'Pop-up' buoyant 'boilie' on short hair
'Drennan' ring
Thin plastic tube with cut-out section,
pushed over and fixed with Superglue
to eye of hook
ANTI-EJECTION RIG
Split shot

ALTERNATIVES TO 'BOILIES'

All these rigs can be fished with baits other than boilies. Hard particles, such as maize, peanuts or tiger nuts, are particularly effective. These baits can be mounted on the hair in exactly the same manner. However, the weight of a large hook when used in conjunction with particles can make the bait behave differently from the free offerings. A remedy, which I first wrote about in 1977, is to push a small piece of polystyrene onto the shank of the hook with the bait. The polystyrene can then be trimmed with a razor blade until it just sinks (see diagram below).

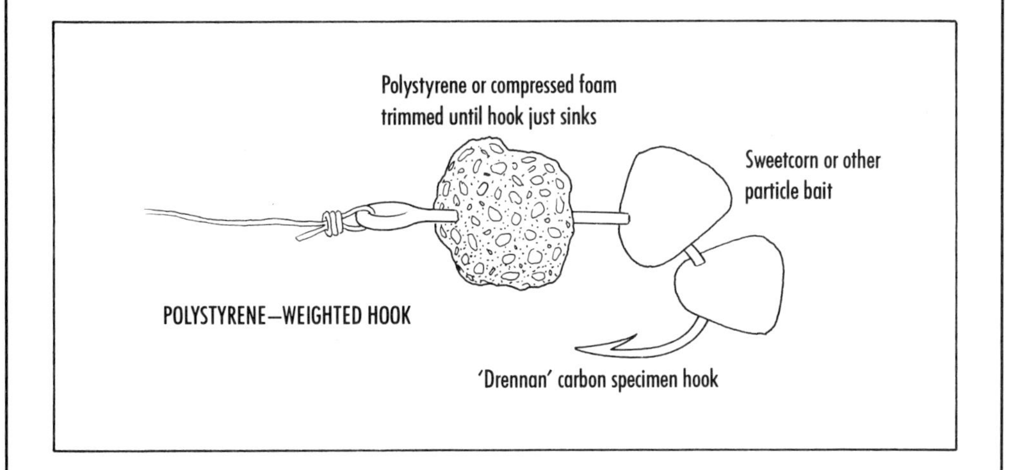

At times, a carp will seem to take a bait just because it is different. Don't ask me why! Some suggest curiosity, others annoyance. Unlikely things do sometimes work, and for no apparent reason: a 'boilie' fished mid-water under a float; a boilie, a peanut and a grain of sweetcorn all fished together on the same hook; a cube of luncheon meat slowly twitched. When the fishing is slow, anything is worth trying. It is easy to become stereotyped as you lie on your bed-chair reading a book, fooling yourself that the fish only feed during the early morning. Somewhere out in the lake there are fish waiting for the right bait fished in the right manner. What you do about it is up to you, but never kid yourself that the fish cannot be caught at a particular time of day, because sooner or later someone will come along and prove you wrong.

Fishing over deep silt can create problems. The use of heavy leads will worsen the difficulties, for the lead will sink deep into the soft bottom. Incorporating a slow-sinking 'fledger' weight helps considerably (see diagram below). This device is not available commercially but is not too difficult to make at home.

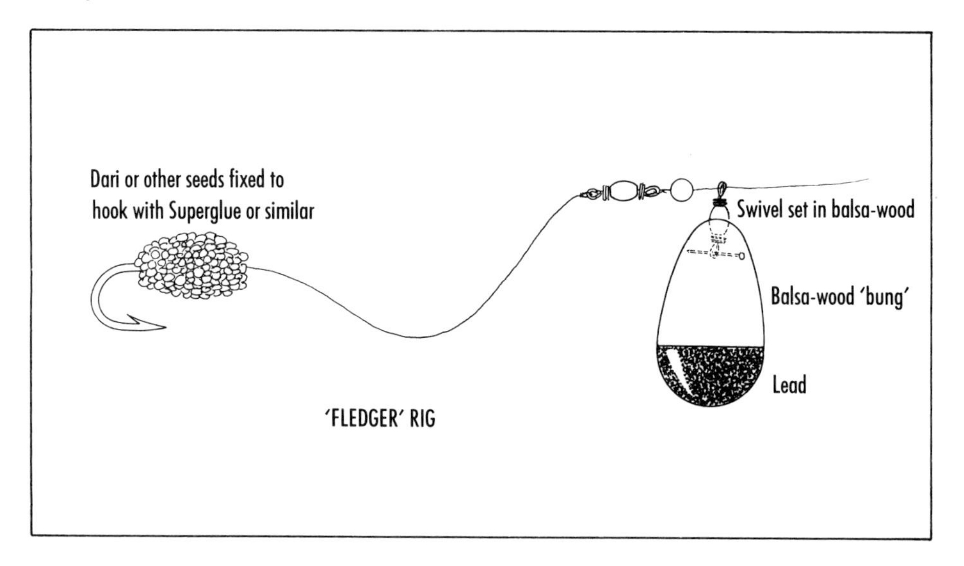

An alternative is to use a paternoster rig (see diagram on page 117). The link between the swivel and the lead should be one and a half to two times the depth of the silt, and a line of a lighter breaking strain should be used to ensure that if the ledger becomes snagged it will break before the main line does. The hook-link can vary in length, but one of 12 in (30 cm) will cover most circumstances.

Most floating baits require the use of a controller if they are to be fished effectively at distance. There are many commercially made products, but a controller is easy enough to construct at home (see diagram on page 117). If you want to fish the surface bait in a fixed position, you can achieve this in a number of ways (see diagrams on page 118). It has long been realized that on hard-fished waters carp do become wary of line on the surface. In the past, this problem was overcome by margin fishing, in which the bait was fished directly below the rod tip. To fish further out, the beachcaster rig was devised (see diagram on page 119), although this is limited to water no deeper than about 10 ft (3 m).

CARP RIGS

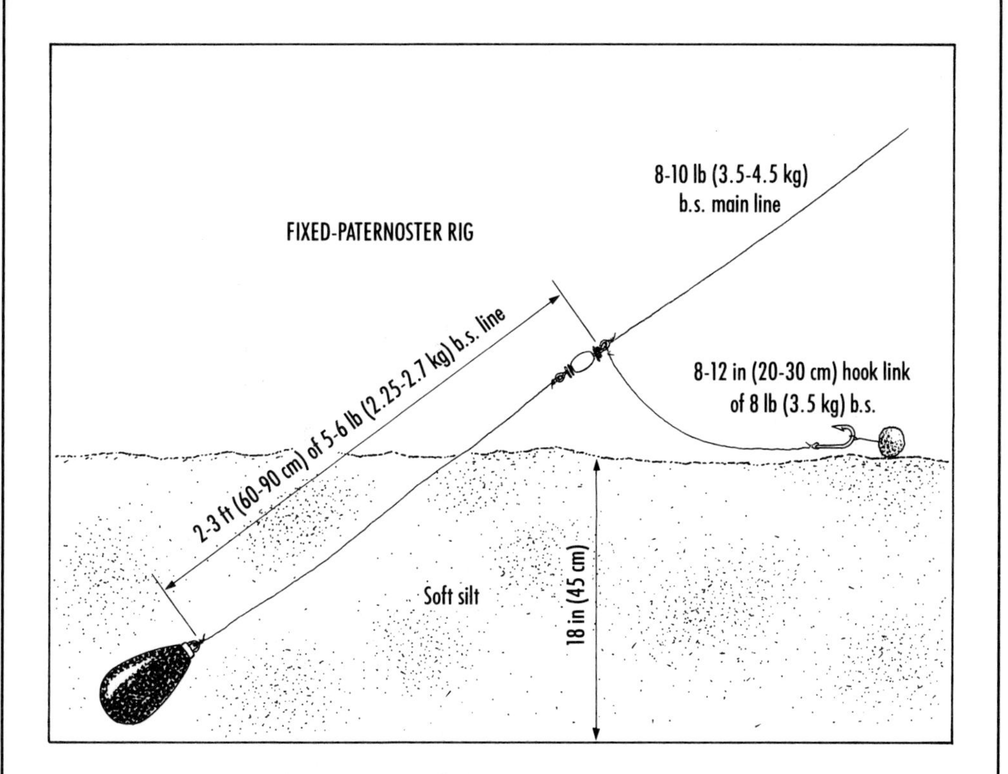
FIXED-PATERNOSTER RIG
8-10 lb (3.5-4.5 kg)
b.s. main line
2-3 ft (60-90 cm) of 5-6 lb (2.25-2.7 kg) b.s. line
8-12 in (20-30 cm) hook link
of 8 lb (3.5 kg) b.s.
Soft silt
18 in (45 cm)

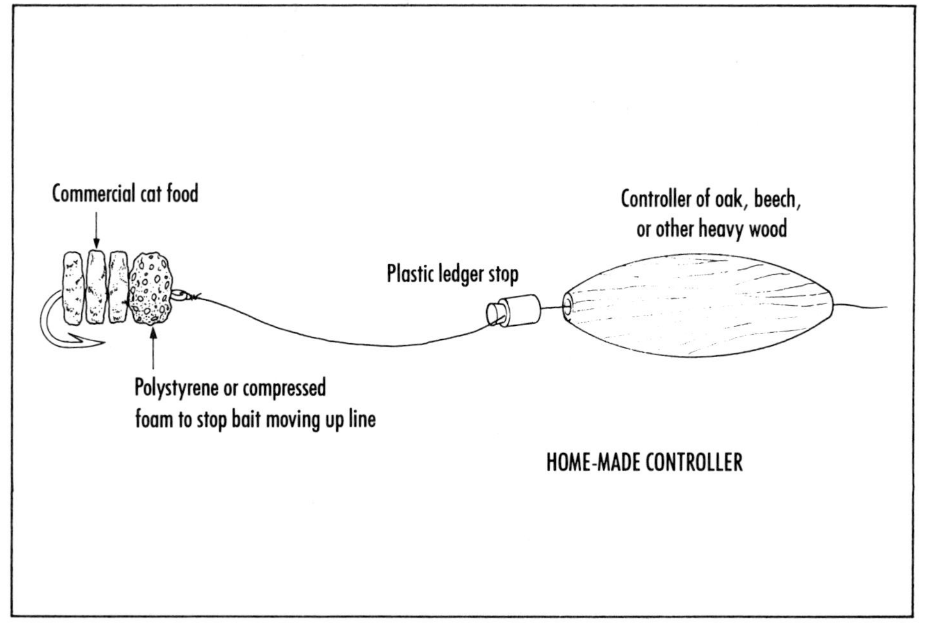
Commercial cat food
Controller of oak, beech,
or other heavy wood
Plastic ledger stop
Polystyrene or compressed
foam to stop bait moving up line
HOME-MADE CONTROLLER

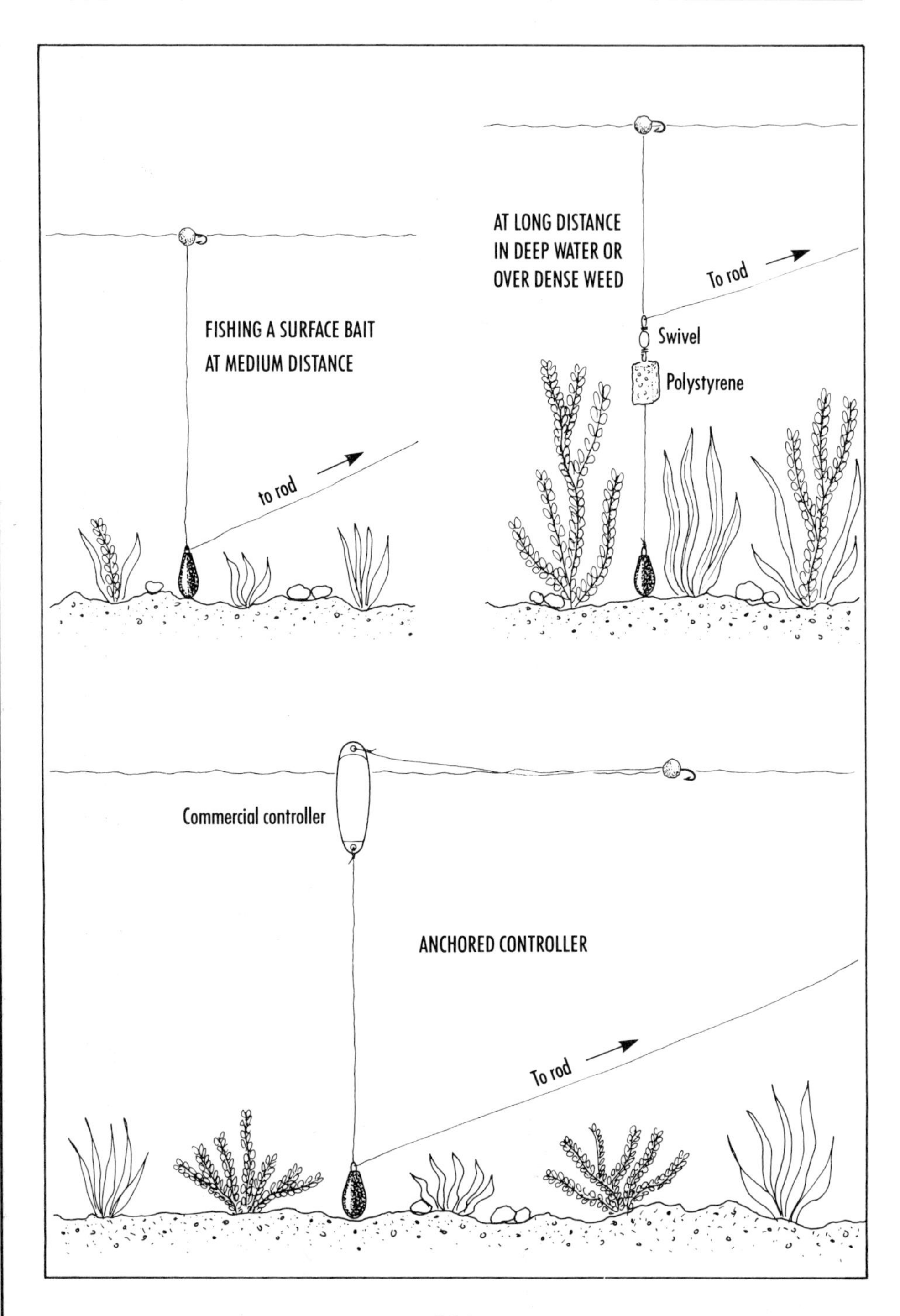
FISHING A SURFACE BAIT
AT MEDIUM DISTANCE
to rod
AT LONG DISTANCE
IN DEEP WATER OR
OVER DENSE WEED
To rod
Swivel
Polystyrene
Commercial controller
ANCHORED CONTROLLER
To rod

Some proprietary surface baits, including Chum Mixer, probably the most popular surface bait for carp, require soaking before use. It is also possible to drill small holes or burn holes with a hot needle through hard or brittle floating particles. Among the most effective floating baits are trout pellets, Go Cat, Munchies, Sugar Puffs, Puffed Wheat and popcorn.

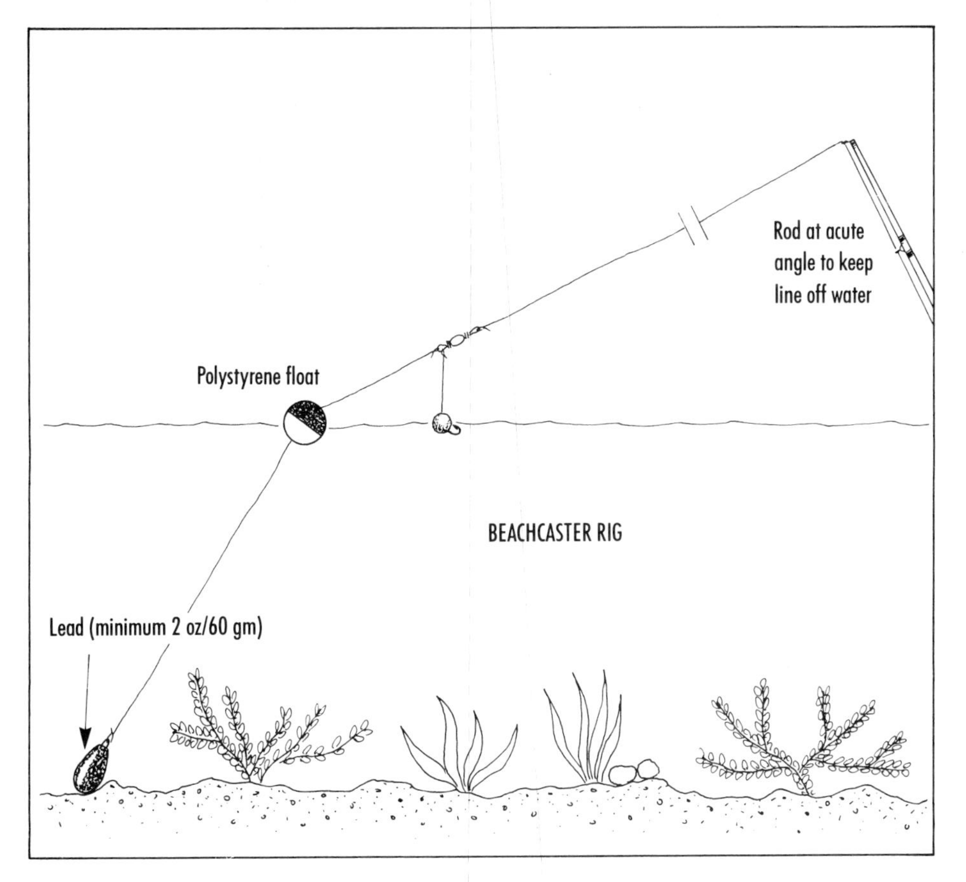

RECOMMENDED KNOTS

Take great care when tying on hooks and swivels. A chain is only as strong as its weakest link and invariably the weakest link in a rig is the knots. The vast majority of carp anglers use eyed hooks and most of those are attached by the five-turn blood knot (see diagrams on page 120). Dick Walker claimed that this knot was unreliable and of

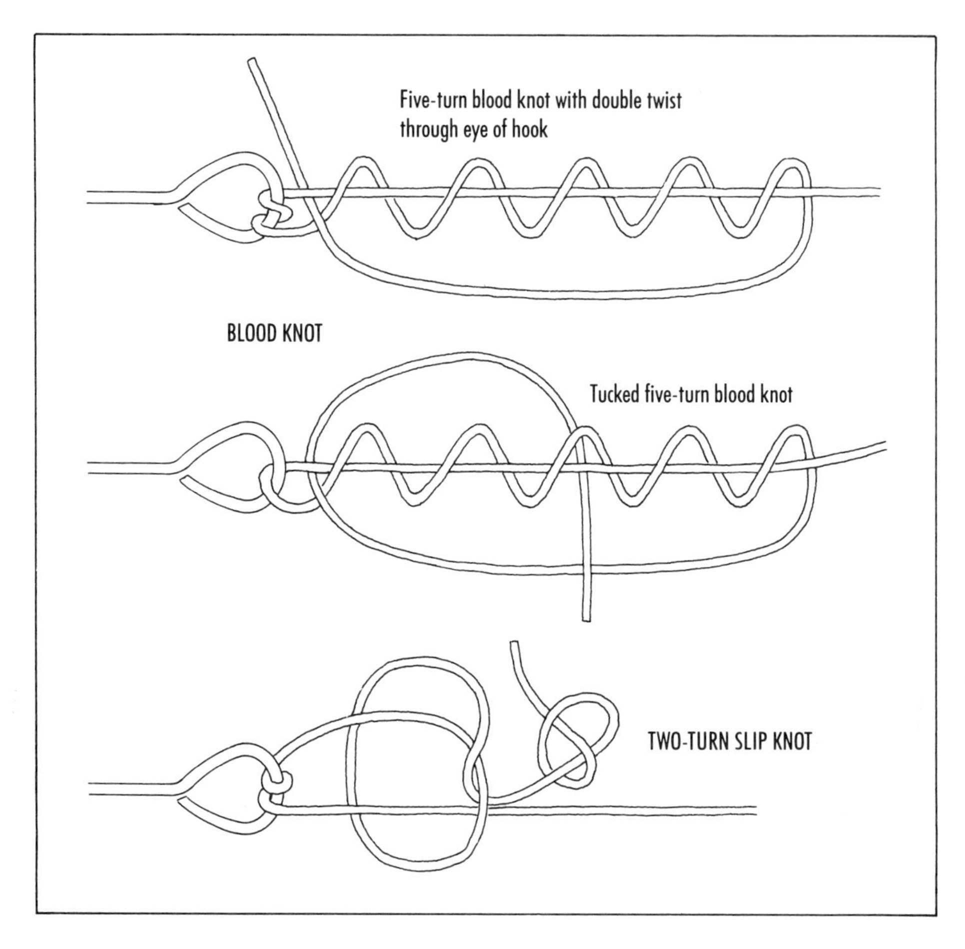

low efficiency, but very successful carp anglers of today, including Andy Little and Kevin Maddocks, recommend it. I have also used it for over twenty years and have never had cause to fault it. However, it is of critical importance to wet all knots (with saliva or water) before pulling them tight. In this way the coils are lubricated when they are forced together into close contact during the final process of tightening, thereby reducing friction and overheating. An alternative knot, highly rated by my former colleagues in the Hallamshire Specimen Group, is the two-turn slip knot (see diagram above). One member, George Sharman, carried out much research on the efficiency of various knots and came to the conclusion that this knot gave the best results, showing almost 100 per cent efficiency.

CHAPTER NINE

WINTER CARP FISHING

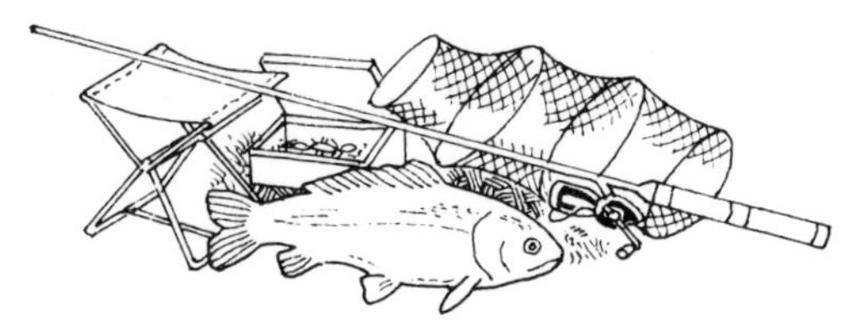

During the 1950s and 1960s Dick Walker was quite adamant that carp fishing during the winter was a waste of time. He wrote, in *Fishing Gazette* in 1959, 'I do not know any water that is not artificially warmed in which big carp can be fished for with much hope of success during the winter months. I should like to be proved wrong, but I think that the view that winter carp fishing is profitless is correct.' In later years he modified his views somewhat, but it was clear that he was still not absolutely convinced. We now know that carp fishing in winter is, without doubt, a practical proposition and by no means only on overstocked, 'hungry' waters. It is rarely easier than it is in summer, but, if you are a little more selective about where and when you fish, the results can compare favourably, even surpass, those obtained during the warmer months.

The most important priority when carp fishing in winter is keeping warm. If you are persistently cold you will not be successful, for you will lack confidence, and without that all is lost. Specialist tackle shops, camping equipment suppliers and army-surplus stores stock the materials you need to keep warm and dry. In addition to your normal equipment you will require a good, waterproof one-piece suit, thermal boots, hat and gloves and the best sleeping bag(s) you can afford. Take plenty of hot drink in a couple of vacuum flasks or adequate facilities for making it on the bank. Some winter nights can be warmer than summer ones, but fishing on an exposed bank in sub-freezing air temperatures, and facing a cutting north-easterly wind with inadequate protection, could lead to hypothermia. If you do get very cold, and start to feel confused and drowsy, immediately pack up and go home. The worst thing you can do is fall asleep.

Winter fishing is usually considered to begin at the start of November, but Britain has had a succession of mild winters in recent

Rod and tackle maker Bill Watson plays a good carp that fell to lobworm and a quivertip on a flooded winter river.

years and perhaps it would be fairer to say it starts when the water temperature has fallen below 10° C (50° F) and has remained there for some time. Often this occurs quite suddenly, and for a period of about ten to fourteen days afterwards, the carp rarely feed. After this acclimatization period the carp settle into a winter feeding regime. Below 10° C (50° F) there is a definite drop in overall activity, although it is noticeable on some waters that activity can increase at temperatures of about 4–6° C (39–43° F). Why this should be so is unclear, although it has been suggested that carp can sense a very cold period developing and have a quick, but relatively intense, feeding spell just beforehand. However, very few carp feed when the water temperature on the bottom of the lake, where the fish are (and not in the margins), falls under 3° C (37° F).

Carp tend to feed for much shorter periods during the winter. A feeding spell may only last for an hour or so in every twenty-four, and often takes place during daylight. Once you can establish what these feeding routines are, you can keep the actual fishing time to a minimum. It is easier to establish these feeding times on waters that hold good stocks of carp and little natural food, and are popular during the summer months. Anglers' baits usually form a substantial part of their diet and this habit can become more pronounced during the winter. Regular bankside disturbance and the carp's repeated capture allow them, in such waters, little opportunity to store up fat reserves. They are therefore at a considerable disadvantage during the winter months if they do not feed. On rich waters where carp can store fat reserves during the summer and autumn, these reserves can be drawn on when it is necessary to forgo feeding. Therefore it can be difficult to predict feeding periods in winter.

Geoff Crawford, who has had considerable success in recent years with his winter fishing, even in the colder weather conditions experienced in the north-east of England, which can average some 3° C (5° F) less than temperatures in the south, offers his observations in the following contribution.

WINTER TACTICS BY GEOFF CRAWFORD

On 'hungry' waters I like to find areas with depths varying between 4 ft and 7 ft (1.2–2 m), if possible near rushes. On many occasions I have seen carp laid up in the vicinity of rushes when the winter sun comes out. A good example of this is one of my local waters which is about 2½ acres (1 hectare) and has a lot of shallow areas and channels to around 7 ft (2 m) deep. One January morning I arrived at about 7 am. The grass was white and crisp and there was a layer of cat-ice over much of the lake. I could see no signs of carp in the ice-free area, which was at the north end. Nevertheless, I started fishing here and set myself a limit of one hour in each swim as I moved towards the southern end of the lake. Gradually a slight, southerly breeze got up and cleared most of the ice away, leaving nearly all the swims fishable.

By 1 pm I had reached the south end of the lake, having seen no indications of carp whatsoever. I again set up and cast my first rod

Redmire Pool in winter. Until as late as the 1970s many thought that carp could not be caught in such conditions. We now know better.

onto a plateau about 3 ft (1 m) deep. My second bait was placed on the edge of a channel in about 4 ft (1.2 m) of water and my third bait was fished in the channel itself, in about 7 ft (2 m) of water. At this stage I was not feeling particularly confident, but decided that the best chance of a take was with the bait in the bottom of the channel. After about half an hour the bait on the plateau was taken and I landed my first fish of the day. I recast to the same area and within an hour I had another good take and landed a fish of similar size. I could not believe that there were numbers of carp laying up on the plateau, in 3 ft (1 m) of water, in these weather conditions. Odd fish must have been drifting in to feed from close by, but exactly where from? I recast my second rod to the edge of some rushes, in about 5 ft (1.5 m) of water, not far from the plateau. It was not long before I had a run on this rod and landed a further fish, and in the last hour before dark I landed four more. On 'rich' waters I have not come across similar situations. The fish seem to behave differently and most of my fish are caught from the deeper areas. I do not know why this is.

Baiting patterns

Since the metabolism of the carp is considerably slower in cold water I use far fewer free offerings than in summer. The cold water also tends to slow down the rate at which the flavour is dispersed from the bait, so I like to increase the flavour level by adding an extra 2 ml per 1 lb (0.4 kg) of bait. I simply add the extra flavouring to the bag of pre-made 'boilies', give the bag a good shake, and allow it to soak in.

I normally introduce about twenty free offerings around each hook bait if I feel really confident, reducing this to about ten if there is a possibility that I might be moving. I used to make my own 'boilies' for winter fishing, adding emulsifiers and various oils, but they seemed to have no benefits and I very rarely bother nowadays. I use Crafty Catcher 'boilies' and have just as much success with them, although most of the various makes of ready-made 'boilies' are excellent. For long-range fishing I use 18 mm (¾ in) 'boilies', which can be cast out a good distance. I always use 'popped-up' or balanced 'boilies' in winter fishing. I prefer the bait off the bottom, because I do not believe that in winter carp are inclined to dig and search for food as they do in summer. Buoyancy is achieved by cutting a 'boilie' in half, hollowing out a space in the middle into which is inserted a 'Polyball', and then using Superglue to stick the two parts back together. This is best done at home and the hook baits can be kept in a separate bag, while those not used during a session can be refrozen for future use.

The rig I use is fairly straightforward. A fixed 2½ oz (70 g) lead, an 8 in (20 cm) Dacron or Kryston Multi-Strand hook link (longer if you are fishing over silt or weed), a small piece of silicon tubing halfway up the shank of the hook and a 'pop-up' or balanced 'boilie' tight up against the bend of the hook.

In winter I try to strike at the slightest movement of the bite indicator. At this time of year carp will often pick up a bait without moving off with it. On small waters I use medium-sized bobbins, and fish with them halfway up the needle. If the wind permits, I cause a slight belly in the line to develop where it enters the water, and watch this for movements. When fishing long range I fish 'tight lines', with the bobbin at the top of the needle, and again strike at any movement. In very adverse conditions it is possible for the line in the Optonic indicator's head to freeze to the wheel and the bobbins to freeze onto the needle, so that small indications will not register. To reduce the risk of freezing, I place my needles directly behind the Optonics and lay a strip of sacking over the top.

A point not covered by Geoff is the effectiveness of different types of bait in winter. It appears that seeds or beans are not as effective in cold weather as they are in summer and, other than 'boilies' and paste baits, nowadays I would use only luncheon meat and sweetcorn. I caught a lot of carp of over 10 lb (4.5 kg) from a long, thin estate lake during the winters of 1975 and 1976 on sweetcorn.

The deepest part of the lake was around the dam area, where there is about 4 ft (1.2 m) of crystal-clear water. The bulk of the carp population of the lake, some forty to fifty fish, could usually be found in this spot. Their normal behaviour was to lie suspended about 1 ft (0.3 m) above the deep silt bed of the lake, occasionally cruising, very slowly, in a big circle to end up back in the same area. It was easy enough to catch them by climbing one of the large, overhanging trees and throwing out a handful of corn close to, but not actually among, the fish.

Usually, it was not long before one of them would gently sidle over and start to suck up the yellow grains. A simple, light float rig, with the shot bunched around the float, and a size 8 hook was all that was required. Over-cast, and reeled back above the fish, the hook bait was soon lying among the free offerings. The strange thing was that although a lot of fish were prepared to feed on bait in this area, it was very rare to see one feed on natural food items.

The only time I found the carp in that lake feeding well in winter was on a very cold late afternoon in January. I just happened to call in for a quick look around as I was passing. I could not see any carp in their usual area around the dam, so I made my way slowly along the bank. It was not until I arrived at the top of the lake, in the extreme shallows, that I found any fish. There were about a dozen feeding intensely, grubbing and rooting about in about 18 in (0.5 m) of water. Fascinated, I watched them until it grew dark, while ice formed all around. This is, of course, very unusual feeding behaviour and what brought it about is impossible to say. There is still much to be understood about the feeding habits and behaviour of carp, particularly in winter.

CHAPTER TEN

FISHING IN EUROPE

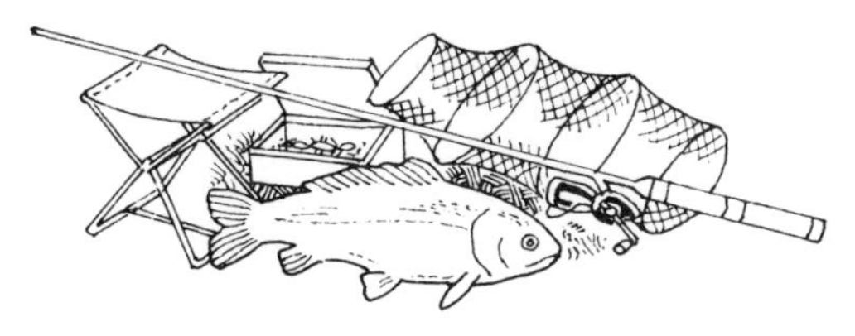

In 1981 I was told that a French angling magazine contained a story about a huge carp. I wrote to the publishers, in Paris, requesting a copy and I was soon looking at photographs of what was probably the largest carp ever caught! The weight of that monster, which was authenticated by the local Brigadier of Police, whose signed affidavit appeared in the article, was 81½ lb (37 kg). It was caught from the Lac de St Cassien, about 10 miles (16 km) west of Cannes, in southern France. Foolishly I never investigated further, but I did mention the fish when I wrote the book 'Redmire Pool'. In September 1984 the book's publisher, Kevin Maddocks, and Paul Regent, of Regent Coaches, visited Cassien for the first time. Their results encouraged Paul to organize fishing trips and this really was the beginning of what has now become an annual exodus of many British carp anglers to France.

The methods used by the British at Cassien resulted in undreamed-of catches of huge carp. Carp of 40 lb (18 kg) and 50 lb (23 kg) were commonplace and fish to over 70 lb (32 kg) have since been caught. It was only a matter of time before other waters were investigated and the potential, not just in France, but in countries such as Holland, Belgium and Spain, was discovered.

Planning a trip

For someone who has never travelled abroad, a foreign fishing trip can be full of pitfalls. The amount of equipment needed for a week's fishing really means that flying is out of the question and the only viable alternative is by road. Travelling in these European countries requires you to drive on the opposite side of the road, and this increases the possibility of an accident. It is essential to have first-class, reliable insurance cover for the vehicle, personal accident, health and your belongings. It is very important to take very good care of your passport, since losing it can cause all sorts of difficulties and delays. Do not carry all your cash, credit cards, traveller's cheques and so on, together, and never leave valuables, including your passport, in an unoccupied vehicle.

It is quite easy to arrange the journey through your local travel agent, or by going to an agency which specializes in angling holidays. Advertisements for these services regularly appear in the angling press.

Probably the best way of travelling to France is to catch the Dover–Calais Hovercraft at about 8 am. The crossing only takes about 1½ hours but no food is available on the boat. The car ferry, on which it is possible to relax and have a meal, is more suitable on the way back, since returning from France usually means that you have already undertaken several hours driving, and a rest is in order.

In France there is the choice of travelling either by the 'Routes Nationales', or 'N' roads, or the 'autoroutes' (motorways). Three factors are involved: cost, time and safety. As for cost, the 'N' roads are toll-free. Using the motorways will cost about £100 in toll fees for the return trip to Cassien.

Using the 'N' roads to Cassien will take more than twenty-four hours. The motorway cuts the journey down to between nine and fifteen hours, depending on speed and stops.

For fishing purposes France is divided into several administrative districts, something like British Water Authority areas. Permits must be obtained for each district and that is all you usually require. For the area which covers Cassien the permit costs about £16 for the year and is available at Pierre's Café at the lakeside. Alternatively, permits can be obtained from tackle shops. Rules are strictly enforced, contrary to the often easy-going attitude sometimes found in Britain. Getting caught breaking the rules in France, and in some of the other European countries, can be very expensive and traumatic, so be warned.

Some relaxation of the rules has recently taken place to accommodate the recent influx of, mainly, British anglers, but night fishing is still not allowed. Undoubtedly some French officials have turned a blind eye to anglers who have broken this law, but in other cases fines have been imposed. Many of the large lakes are used as holiday resorts and become very crowded, especially during August, when most of the nation takes its annual holiday. Serious fishing is a waste of time then.

Food and other costs

Provisions are best obtained from the supermarkets and the cost, for most essentials apart from meat, is similar to that in Britain. But eating out, even in a modest café, is expensive. Good-quality tackle is either very expensive or non-existent. Make sure you carry adequate supplies of line, hooks, beads and swivels as losses on snags can be considerable. Take some tools for possible vehicle repairs and the obvious spares, such as fan belts and distributor points. Hire vehicles are unbelievably costly, at around £500 per week.

Bear in mind when looking for new still-waters that many of the 'blue patches on the map' will have very poor access roads. There really is no need to visit the popular waters, and anyway it is much more pleasant to find a secluded carp water and have it to yourself. In France there is no shortage of these. The vast majority of the carp have never been caught, so sophisticated methods and baits are not usually necessary. In some of the waters the carp breed very successfully, so that there are lots of small-to-medium-sized fish. Many of the rivers in France also have good stocks of carp, some of them monsters. The larger fish in the rivers tend to come from the slower, deeper stretches. A river which has recently become popular with English anglers, is the River Lot where it is dammed and widens out at St Geniez d'Olt, north-east of Rodez.

A fair number of carp waters in France hold big populations of crayfish. Undoubtedly the carp feed on these, but they can be a nuisance at times. On some waters in southern France, a huge crayfish population would demolish a 'boilie' in about half an hour. You need to fish the hook bait as a 'pop-up' to keep it away from these pests. It has been suggested that by attracting large numbers of crayfish into the fishing area you might, in turn, encourage carp to begin feeding. That may or may not be the case, so I try and get the best of both worlds by initially introducing a large quantity of maize to hold the carp, and then regularly putting in small quantities of 'boilies'.

If you are looking for monster carp in France, one thing to

remember is that a lot of the lakes are formed by damming rivers. Every few years many of these lakes are drained down for maintenance work and a lot of the carp are lost.

Carp fishing in Holland

Although the carp in Holland do not grow as large as in France, the carp fishing is fabulous. There is water everywhere, the majority of it stocked with fish attaining similar sizes to those found in Britain. The Dutch people are usually very friendly and helpful to visiting British anglers and, as many of them speak English, language difficulties seldom crop up. Unlike many of the British, they do not leave litter in their towns and countryside, so please do not abuse their hospitality and endanger the present good relations.

The Twente canal is very popular with British carp anglers and has produced carp to over 40 lb (18 kg), but the whole country is a maze of drains and canals, most of which hold good stocks of carp. There are thousands of ponds and lakes, many of which are small (up to 5 acres/2 hectares) and intimate. The control of the fishing rights is similar to that found in Britain, the vast majority of the waters being controlled by fishing clubs, whose charges are very modest. The average cost is about £1 per day, £3 per week and £10 per year. Fishing tickets are usually available from the local pub, or the local Town Hall or Police Station will advise you. On rivers and canals which have boat traffic, fishing is free but only one rod is allowed, unlike other waters, where a maximum of two is permitted. Before fishing, a national rod licence must be purchased, costing about £3.50 per person and valid for one year. This allows you to fish with a maximum of two rods, apart from on the navigable rivers and canals, and is available from any Post Office. There is no close season but night fishing is only allowed during June, July and August.

Another reason why carp fishing in Europe is so popular with British anglers is the abundance of 'common' carp, which are very localized in Britain. Most of the other European countries, including Belgium, Germany, Italy and Spain, have a great number of waters holding vast stocks of big carp which have hardly been exposed to the very successful British carp-fishing methods. In most of the European countries some absolutely unbelievable fishing awaits those with the pioneering spirit.

CHAPTER ELEVEN

RESPONSIBILITY AND BEHAVIOUR

There are, I am happy to say, encouraging signs that the majority of carp anglers in Britain are not prepared to tolerate the behaviour of a destructive few and things are improving. Sometimes it is a question of ignorance, although there are undoubtedly a few anglers who knowingly fail to treat the fish they catch with care and respect. There is a tendency for carp anglers to use as fine a line as is possible, and often for good reason, but this does tend to prolong the time taken to subdue the fish and land it. It also, of course, increases the chance that the fish may become snagged and break free. The majority of my fishing is carried out with lines with a breaking strain of between 8 lb (3.5 kg) and 15 lb (7 kg) and on a few exceptional occasions I have dropped down to 6 lb (2.7 kg). It is wrong, however, even on totally open, snag-free waters to use very fine lines in an attempt to increase bites. In recent years some anglers have resorted to using ridiculously fine lines, of 2 lb (0.9 kg) and 3 lb (1.35 kg) breaking strain, fished in conjunction with Power Gum elastic, which reduces the chance of direct breakage.

I have it on good authority that large carp have been played for over an hour by users of this method. Prolonged forced swimming in carp can cause substantial changes in the biochemistry of the muscle and blood. Excessive exercise results in energy being produced by glycolysis. In this process stored carbohydrate, as glycogen, is converted into glucose, then into pyruvate and finally into lactate without the use of oxygen. The lactate accumulates, mostly in the muscle tissue, until oxygen becomes available and can be therefore looked upon as an oxygen 'debt'. At best excessive levels of lactate

Len Arbery stalking the monsters of Redmire.

can be dealt with by excretion but this would mean that the fish would be throwing away over 90 per cent of the energy contained in the original glucose. At worst such lactate levels could cause death.

The fact that fish subjected to these extremely long periods of being played are then taken out of the water to be unhooked, weighed and photographed can only result in additional stress, making the viability of the carp even more doubtful. Since such light-line tactics are highly dangerous to the welfare of the fish, they should be abhorrent to any caring angler.

It is now widely accepted that on popular fisheries some carp are caught several times a season. During its lifetime a fish could therefore be caught thirty or more times. It is of paramount importance, because of these repeated captures, that fish should be treated with the utmost care. Damage, and excessive stress, will not only have a direct effect upon the future health, longevity and growth rate of a carp, but will also determine how easy it is to catch in the future. If the fish is highly stressed or damaged (which will in itself cause stress) during capture, it will associate this experience with the act of picking up the bait. All anglers, therefore, have a selfish motive for ensuring that being caught is as unstressful as possible for the fish.

Once the fish is in the landing net it is important to give it an opportunity to recover, in the water, from its physical exertions. How would you feel, if after running until you were exhausted, someone then stuck your head in a plastic bag so that you could not breathe? If you are fishing with a friend, get him to hold the carp in the landing net until you have all your equipment ready to unhook, weigh and photograph it. If you are alone, immediately put the fish in a carp sack for a few minutes until you are ready. The carp should then be taken from the water and laid on a soft surface. This can be long grass which you have already wetted, a couple of damp carp sacks, a piece of wet carpet underlay or, ideally, an unhooking mat. Then gently, but firmly, unhook the fish.

A few quick photographs can be taken before the fish is laid on an already prepared, wet, open weigh bag. The fish is quickly weighed with scales that have been 'zeroed' against the bag and is then carried to the water's edge without being removed from the bag. This procedure keeps handling, and the time the fish is out of the water, to a minimum and causes little discomfort. When holding the fish for photographs, avoid fancy poses. Your movements should be slow and precise, for quick, jerky movements will frighten and disturb the fish and cause it to flap and wriggle. Kneel on the ground, holding the fish close to your chest just above the unhooking mat. Then, if it happens to slip from your grasp, it will not be harmed.

Carp sacks

I dislike retaining fish in carp sacks. Admittedly they are the most humane method so far devised, but they still have drawbacks. There is obviously some restriction of water transfer and therefore under no circumstances should more than one carp ever be put in a single sack. I firmly believe that if a fish is quickly returned to the water after being caught, it soon forgets the incident and the effect upon its future behaviour is minimal. However, the longer it is retained in a sack the greater is the impression made upon the fish of the stressful experience of being caught.

I accept that there are circumstances in which an angler catches a big fish, for example when alone at night or in extreme weather conditions, when using a sack is necessary. Carp retained for several hours in sacks do recover much of their vigour and are difficult to handle, sometimes damaging themselves while on the bank. In such a situation, when the carp is first removed from the water, I leave it in the sack and lay it on a weigh mat or a piece of carpet underlay. I check that its fins are not bent – otherwise if it flaps it could break them – and lay a further wet carp sack over it. I leave it alone for three or four minutes before I attempt to remove it from the sack.

Some rules often appear petty and unreasonable. That may very well be the case, but the fishing club may have had the rules imposed on it by the fishery owner, and if those rules are broken it may result in the loss of the fishing. Sometimes silly regulations are imposed by clubs and Water Authorities who have little understanding of specialist fishing. Obvious examples are restrictions on the number of rods allowed and various bait bans. But I have found that most fishing clubs and associations are only too eager to allow you to assist in the decision-making and running of their organization. Once they realize that you are a reasonable chap, and if you put your case well, they will listen to your arguments, and often accept what you say. All Water Authorities have a duty to make provision for, and heed the views of, fishery consultative associations. Anyone with an interest in a fishery is eligible to make his opinions known to the Water Authority through these organizations. If you can get the consultative body to pass a resolution asking the Water Authority to change a particular bye-law, then that revision stands a very good chance of taking place.

If you care about carp fishing and want to protect its future you have to become 'involved' in some way. You may have found yourself a nice little niche, a private water perhaps, where you feel that you have nothing to worry about. But very few situations remain the same for long. Lakes are purchased by developers or other water users, and the threat of pollution is never far away. It is therefore no good burying your head in the sand.

CHAPTER TWELVE

A GUIDE TO CARP WATERS IN BRITAIN

The following list is my personal choice of carp waters that combine reliable sport with accessibility. I have not included waters where access is limited because of long waiting lists or control by a syndicate, or waters that are notoriously difficult.

A1 PIT, Newark-on-Trent, Nottinghamshire. Adjacent to the A1 roadbridge spanning the River Trent, this large, open gravel pit of about 40 acres (16 hectares) holds a good head of carp to over 20 lb (9 kg). A fair number of common carp are also present. Day tickets are available on the bank.

ANGLER'S PARADISE FISHING HOLIDAYS, Halwill Junction, Beaworthy, Devon. This complex of 8 lakes, the largest about 4 acres (1·5 hectares), holds plenty of carp. The stock and size vary in each lake, those waters with the most stock being the easiest to fish. Some of the carp are over 20 lb (9 kg). The lakes are part of a 50-acre (20 hectares) estate offering self-catering holiday accommodation with fishing. Details from Zyg Gregorek. Telephone: 040922–559.

BOOTON CLAY PIT, near Reepham, Norfolk. This 4-acre (1·5 hectares) clay pit holds a small head of big carp. Fish to 35 lb (16 kg) have been reported in recent years. Day tickets are available on the bank. The fishing is controlled by the Aylsham and District AA.

BRAYTON POND, near Aspatria, Cumbria. This water holds what are reputed to be genuine wild carp, averaging about 4 lb (1·8 kg). Some larger fish of over 12 lb (5·5 kg) have been caught from this shallow (no more than 4 ft/1·2 m deep) 8-acre (3 hectares) lake. Crucian carp are also present and some match fishing takes place, at which time the pond can be fully booked up. Day tickets are available at the farm from the owner, Mr Ward. Telephone: 0965–262.

BROADLANDS LAKE, Ower, near Romsey, Southampton, Hampshire. This large gravel pit, created in 1977 during the construction of the M27, holds a large stock of carp. The majority of the fish weigh up to 20 lb (9 kg), but in 1988 a fish weighing 35 lb (16 kg) was introduced and was later caught. Day and season permits are available from the fishery manager, Mr M. Simmonds. Telephone: 0703–733167 or 869881.

BROOKLANDS LAKE, Dartford, Kent. Situated next to the A2, this 28-acre (11·5 hectares) gravel pit contains a huge stock of carp. Most of these are between 10 lb and 20 lb (4·5–9 kg), but a few are present of around 30 lb (14 kg). Day tickets are available on the bank. No night fishing is allowed. This water is under a lot of angling pressure and bankside space is at a premium. Details from the Secretary, Dartford and District APS, 29 Berkeley Crescent, Dartford, Kent.

BURTON MERE, Burton Manor, near Chester, Merseyside. This 3-acre (1 hectare) long-established estate lake has recently been given a new lease of life. It now contains an excellent head of carp to 25 lb (11·5 kg). Day tickets are available from Rod and Tackle, Enfield Road, Ellesmere Port, Merseyside. Telephone: 051–356–0678.

BYSINGWOOD, Bysingwood Road, Faversham, Kent. A very heavily stocked water, with the odd fish of just over 20 lb (9 kg). Details of club membership from the Secretary, Faversham AC, 5 Kennedy Close, Faversham, Kent. Telephone: 0795–533240.

CAPESTHORNE HALL, Capesthorne Estate, Capesthorne, Macclesfield, Cheshire. Lying close to the A34 north of Siddington, the estate lake, spanned by a bridge, holds some excellent carp. These include about six of over 20 lb (9 kg), the biggest around 28 lb (13 kg). Season permits for the lake can be obtained from the Secretary, Stoke-on-Trent AS, 5 Kingsfield Oval, Basford, Stoke-on-Trent ST4 6HN. A small ¼-acre (0·1 hectare) pond, known as the STOCK POND, is close to the estate lake and holds a good head of small carp. This can be fished on a day ticket obtainable from the bailiff, Mr A. Bradford, by telephoning 861–584.

CHAPEL BOATING LAKE, Chapel St Leonards, near Skegness, Lincolnshire. This 2½-acre (1 hectare) fishery holds a good head of carp to just over 20 lb (9 kg). The lake is close to the sea and serious carp fishing is difficult apart from during the early morning. Day tickets available on site. Information from the owner, Mr J. Cook. Telephone: 0754–72631.

CHESTERFORD FISHERIES, Great Chesterford, Saffron Walden, Essex. Not far from junction 9 on the M11, this site comprises three mature gravel pits totalling about 13 acres (5·5 hectares). They offer carp fishing of a very high standard with fish to over 30 lb (14 kg). Season permits are available, but are not cheap, from Paul Elsegood, 2 Wentfords Cottages, Clare Road, Poslingford, Sudbury, Suffolk.

COLLEGE RESERVOIR, near Falmouth, Cornwall. With access from the B3291, this large water covering about 40 acres (16 hectares) holds around 200–250 carp of over 10 lb (4·5 kg), with perhaps a dozen of over 20 lb (9 kg) and one fish of around 30 lb (14 kg). The fishing is controlled by the South West Water Authority, Peninsula House, Rydon Lane, Exeter, Devon. Telephone: 0392–219666. Night fishing is not normally allowed, but day tickets can be obtained from a machine in the Argal car park.

CUTTLE MILL, Wilshaw, North Warwickshire. Situated off the A4091, near the National Golf Centre, are two waters of about 3 acres (1 hectare) each, containing a large head of carp of over 10 lb (4·5 kg) and some of over 20 lb (9 kg). Fishing is allowed from 6.45 am until dusk and day tickets are available on site. This is a very popular and prolific fishery, producing around 3000 fish of 10–20 lb (4·5–9 kg) each season. Details from Tony Higgins by telephoning 0827–872253.

CUTT MILL, Elstead, near Farnham, Surrey. A famous and popular carp water covering about 8 acres (3 hectares). This attractive estate lake holds a good head of carp, including some of over 20 lb (9 kg). Details of club membership from the Secretary, Farnham AS, 70 Prince Charles Crescent, Farnborough, Hampshire.

DARENTH, Dartford, Kent. Four gravel pits varying in size from 3 acres (1 hectare) to 13 acres (5 hectares). A very popular water holding some big carp, including fish of over 30 lb (14 kg). Night fishing is allowed. A Leisure Sport permit-only water. Details from Leisure Sport Angling, Thorpe Park, Staines Lane, Chertsey, Surrey. Telephone: 09328–64872.

ELSTOW PIT, Elstow, Bedfordshire. Just off the A6, this 30-acre (12 hectares) clay pit holds a good head and size range of carp to about 26 lb (12 kg). It is controlled by the Stewartby AC, which offers season permits.

FARLOW'S, Iver Lane, near Iver, Buckinghamshire. This mature gravel pit has a long history of producing big carp and specimen fish of other species. The lake record is 37¼ lb (17 kg) and the fish was caught twice in October 1983. Day tickets are available from the office at the lake. The water is controlled by William Bower Fishing, who allow night fishing.

GEEN'S PIT, Shropham, near Snetterton, Norfolk. A small, shallow pit of about one acre (0·5 hectare). The water holds only a handful of carp but fish of well over 30 lb (14 kg) have been taken. Fishing by prior arrangement with the owner, Mr Geen. Telephone: 095383–735.

GREY MIST MERE, Woolston, near Warrington, Cheshire. This long-established carp fishery of about 10 acres (4 hectares) holds large stocks of small to medium-sized carp. Club membership details from Warrington Anglers' Association, 23 Nora Street, Warrington, Cheshire.

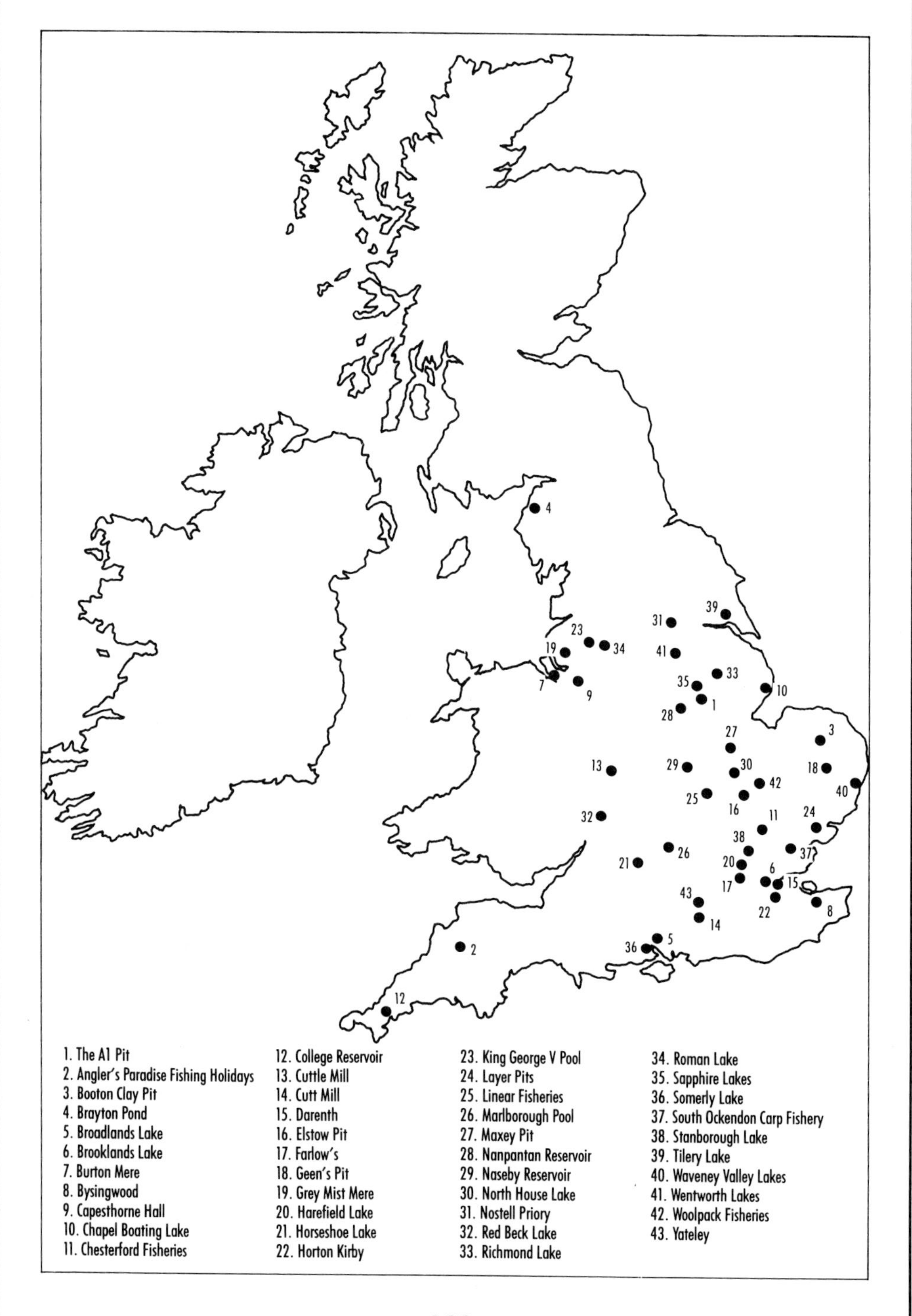
1. The A1 Pit
2. Angler's Paradise Fishing Holidays
3. Booton Clay Pit
4. Brayton Pond
5. Broadlands Lake
6. Brooklands Lake
7. Burton Mere
8. Bysingwood
9. Capesthorne Hall
10. Chapel Boating Lake
11. Chesterford Fisheries
12. College Reservoir
13. Cuttle Mill
14. Cutt Mill
15. Darenth
16. Elstow Pit
17. Farlow's
18. Geen's Pit
19. Grey Mist Mere
20. Harefield Lake
21. Horseshoe Lake
22. Horton Kirby
23. King George V Pool
24. Layer Pits
25. Linear Fisheries
26. Marlborough Pool
27. Maxey Pit
28. Nanpantan Reservoir
29. Naseby Reservoir
30. North House Lake
31. Nostell Priory
32. Red Beck Lake
33. Richmond Lake
34. Roman Lake
35. Sapphire Lakes
36. Somerly Lake
37. South Ockendon Carp Fishery
38. Stanborough Lake
39. Tilery Lake
40. Waveney Valley Lakes
41. Wentworth Lakes
42. Woolpack Fisheries
43. Yateley

HAREFIELD LAKE, Moorhall Road, Harefield, Middlesex. The entrance is opposite the Halfway House, not far from the entrance to Savay Lake (see below). This 40-acre (16 hectares) gravel pit holds a large number of big carp but is heavily fished by some of the best carp specialists in the country. It is a very difficult water but the rewards can be great. The lake is still being worked and is gradually increasing in size. The fishing is controlled by William Bower Fishing, Trout Road, West Drayton, Middlesex. Telephone: 0895–444707.

HORSESHOE LAKE, Lechlade, Gloucestershire. As its name implies, this large 80-acre (32 hectares) gravel pit is shaped like a horseshoe. It is conveniently located next to the A361, just north of Lechlade. The fishery has a tremendous stock of carp offering good sport, although at present there are not many of over 15 lb (7 kg). The lake is also used for sailing. Day tickets are available from Mr A. Chase, The Paper Shop, Burford Road, Lechlade, Gloucestershire. Tickets must be obtained before fishing. The water is controlled by Amey Anglers Association, who offer season permits. Details from the Fisheries Officer, ARC, Besselsleigh Road, Wootton, Abingdon, Oxfordshire. Telephone: 0865–730851.

HORTON KIRBY, Horton Kirby, near Dartford, Kent. Three heavily stocked gravel pits stocked with carp of all sizes up to about 25 lb (11·5 kg). Day tickets are available on the bank.

KING GEORGE V POOL, Altrincham, Cheshire. This shallow 3-acre (1 hectare) pond is heavily stocked with carp which are mainly small. Day tickets are available on the bank from the bailiff.

LAYER PITS, Colchester, Essex. This 25-acre (10 hectares) water holds large stocks of carp, including plenty of over 10 lb (4·5 kg) and some older fish to 35 lb (16 kg). It also holds some big bream. Season permits are available from the Secretary, Colchester Angling Preservation Society, 36 Winsley Road, Colchester, Essex.

LINEAR FISHERIES, Little Linford Lane, Milton Keynes, Buckinghamshire. This complex of gravel pits, totalling some 300 acres (120 hectares), provides some excellent carp fishing. A variety of waters offer syndicate, season, and day-ticket membership for the carp fishing, which varies from easy to difficult. Carp to over 30 lb (14 kg) have been caught. Details from Len Gurd, Linear House, 2 Northcroft, Shenley Lodge, Milton Keynes, Buckinghamshire. Telephone: 0908–607577.

MARLBOROUGH POOL, near Witney, Oxfordshire. Situated close to the A40, this well-established gravel pit holds a good head of carp. The fishery is very popular and has seen a lot of attention. Details of club membership from the Secretary, Oxford and District AA, 18 Linden Road, Bicester, Oxfordshire.

MAXEY PIT, Deeping St James, Peterborough, Northamptonshire. This 6-acre (2·5 hectares) gravel pit is heavily stocked with carp of over 10 lb (4·5 kg). Day tickets can be obtained from Mr N. Cesare, 55 Cardinals Gate, Werrington, Peterborough. Telephone: 0733–70226.

NANPANTAN RESERVOIR, Nanpantan, near Loughborough, Leicestershire. Adjacent to the B5350, this small, open fishery of about 6 acres (2·5 hectares) contains a fair head of carp of around 8 lb (3·5 kg), and a few larger fish. The water is controlled by Severn–Trent Water Authority. Details from Mr W. Wortley, 45 Baxter Gate, Loughborough, Leicestershire. Telephone: 0509–212697.

NASEBY RESERVOIR, Naseby, near Daventry, Northamptonshire. This 50-acre (20 hectares) water promises to be a tremendous carp fishery in the near future. A few years ago the reservoir was drained and the coarse fish removed. It was then restocked with carp which are growing at an excellent rate. Many of the fish are now approaching 10 lb (4·5 kg) and there are a few bigger fish already present. Access is from the A50 north of Thornby. Season permits are available from the British Waterways Board, Willow Grange, Church Road, Watford WD1 3QA. Telephone: 0923–226422.

NORTH HOUSE LAKE, Wyboston, St Neots, Cambridgeshire. Close to the A1, this 5-acre (2 hectares) gravel pit holds around sixty carp to 23 lb (10·5 kg), with most of the fish over 10 lb (4·5 kg). Season permits, costing about £7.50, are available from the Secretary, Luton AC, 18 The Hedgerows, Parkside, Furzton, Milton Keynes MK4 1BP or from Leslie's Tackle Shop, 89 Park Street, Luton, Bedfordshire.

NOSTELL PRIORY, near Wakefield, Yorkshire. The middle water of this chain of three lakes is a well-stocked carp fishery holding fish to over 20 lb (9 kg). Day and season permits are available from the fishing lodge. Details from Mr J. Austerfield. Telephone: 0924–863562.

RED BECK LAKE, Evesham, Hereford and Worcester. This very heavily stocked pond, of about 4 acres (1·5 hectares), is an easy water in which to catch carp. They do not reach a large size, with the vast majority of the fish under 2 lb (0·9 kg), but it can be an ideal place to learn. Enquiries and season permits from Peter Mohan, Cypryvan, Bedford Road, Lower Stondon, Bedfordshire SG16 6EA. Telephone: 0462–816370.

RICHMOND LAKE, North Hykeham, Near Lincoln, Lincolnshire. A large gravel pit close to the A46, this water holds good stocks of carp to over 20 lb (9 kg). Day tickets and season permits are available on site.

ROMAN LAKES, near Marple, Cheshire. A well-stocked, shallow lake holding carp to about 20 lb (9 kg). There is a fun park open to the general public, which creates some problems for anglers. Day tickets available from the café adjacent to the lake.

SAPPHIRE LAKES, Norwell Lane, Cromwell, near Newark-on-Trent, Nottinghamshire. This is a prolific fishery with a good number of carp of over 10 lb (4·5 kg) and some larger. Fish to over 25 lb (11·5 kg) are caught most seasons. Night fishing is allowed and permits cost £2 per day. Contact Ken Barker on 0636–821131.

SOMERLY LAKE, near Ringwood, Hampshire. A mature gravel pit of about 15 acres (6 hectares) that holds good stocks of carp, including several of over 20 lb (9 kg). Day tickets are available on the bank.

SOUTH OCKENDON CARP FISHERIES, near South Ockendon, Essex. The site comprises three gravel pits, each of about 3 acres (1 hectare), which are well stocked with carp to about 25 lb (11·5 kg). Day tickets are available on the bank. Further details from Mr T. Coster. Telephone: 0702–342148.

STANBOROUGH LAKE, Welwyn Garden City, Hertfordshire. This gravel pit of about 20 acres (8 hectares) holds an excellent stock of carp, some of them topping 20 lb (9 kg). The best reported fish weighed 27 lb (12 kg). Day tickets are available on the bank. One rod only allowed before 1 November.

TILERY LAKE, Broomfleet, North Humberside. This large, open clay pit of 27 acres (11 hectares) contains an excellent stock of big carp and is probably the best big-carp water in the North-East. The lake holds about 100 carp, the majority nearing 20 lb (9 kg), with a good proportion of fish over that weight. The lake record is 27 lb (12 kg). Fishing is controlled by the Hull and District AA, which issues season permits that are available direct or from local tackle shops. Night fishing is limited and details are available from D. Littleproud, 13 Sawston Avenue, Hull, North Humberside HU5 5RP. Telephone: 0482–564808.

WAVENEY VALLEY LAKES, Wortwell, near Harleston, Norfolk. This is a very famous and popular complex of lakes with caravan accommodation. The site comprises eight lakes ranging from 2 to 5 acres (1–2 hectares) and holding good stocks of big carp. There are lots of carp of over 10 lb (4·5 kg) and a fair sprinkling of twenty-pounders (9 kg). The best fish weighed 36 lb (16·5 kg). Day tickets are available from the site shop or the bailiffs. Night fishing is allowed. Information on 098–686–530.

WENTWORTH LAKES, Wentworth Park, Wentworth, near Sheffield, South Yorkshire. Access is from the B6089 to this series of lakes run by Sheffield and District AA. A reasonable stock of carp exists, with many over 10 lb (4·5 kg).

There are some nice common carp present. A few fish of over 20 lb (9 kg) exist, the best being around 28 lb (13 kg). There is no night fishing. Details from the Secretary, Sheffield District AA, Station Hotel, The Wicker, Sheffield 3.

WOOLPACK FISHERIES, Cow Lane, near Hilton, St Ives, Cambridgeshire. This chain of gravel pits contains probably eight which hold good stocks of carp, including some 'commons', to well over 20 lb (9 kg). Season permits are available from Bill Chillingworth, The Cottage, St Peters Street, Caxton, Cambridgeshire. Telephone: 09544–593.

YATELEY, Sandhurst Road, Yateley, near Camberley, Surrey. This very famous complex of attractive gravel pits holds some monster carp. They are very difficult to catch, having received a lot of attention. The 12-acre (5 hectares) Match Lake holds good stocks of carp, including some of over 20 lb (9 kg). The 5-acre (2 hectares) Corpse Lake has a handful of big carp, including a thirty-pounder (14 kg). The 9-acre (3.5 hectares) Car Park Lake holds a few big carp, and produced a forty-two pounder (19 kg) some years ago, although this fish is almost certainly dead. The 13-acre (5 hectares) North Lake also holds a few big carp, including a fish that is well over 40 lb (18 kg). Season permits are available but are limited. Apply to Leisure Sport Angling, Thorpe Park, Staines Lane, Chertsey, Surrey. Telephone: 09328–64872.

INDEX

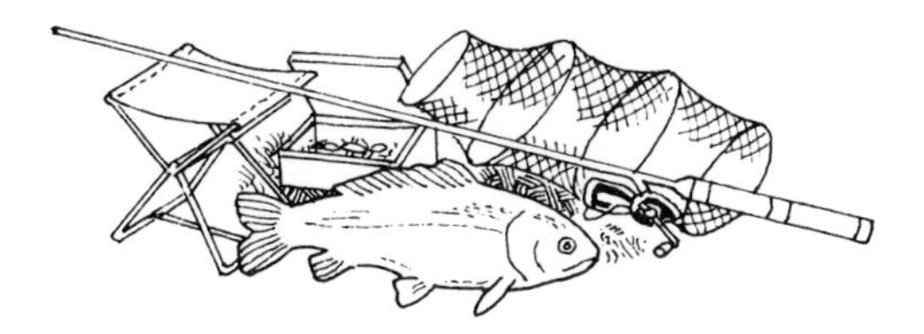

Page numbers in italics refer to illustrations

Photography Acknowledgments
Colour: Following page 32*: Kevin Clifford; Len Head; P&S Ward/Natural Science Photos; Kevin Clifford; Kevin Clifford.* Following page 48*: Bruce Pockington/Natural Science Photos; Trevor Housby; Kevin Clifford; Kevin Cifford; Jim Tyree.* Following page 80*: Jim Tyree; Jim Tyree; Kevin Clifford; P&S Ward/Natural Science Photos.* Following page 96*: Kevin Clifford; Len Head; Kevin Clifford; Kevin Clifford.*
Black and White*: All black and white photographs by Kevin Clifford except for: page 82 Frank Lane Picture Agency; page 103 Graeme Pullen; pages 107 and 132 Len Arbery.*